Risk of Impaired Condition of Watersheds Containing National Forest Lands

Thomas C. Brown and Pamela Froemke

Abstract

We assessed the risk of impaired condition of the nearly 3700 5th-level watersheds in the contiguous 48 states containing the national forests and grasslands that make up the U.S. Forest Service's National Forest System (NFS). The assessment was based on readily available, relatively consistent nationwide data sets for a series of indicators representing watershed stressors and resources at risk of watershed impairment. Using a set of weights that express the relative importance of the indicators, a summary measure of relative risk of watershed impairment was computed for each entire watershed, each NFS part of each watershed, and each non-NFS part of each watershed. The summary measure reflects the assumption that indicators are linearly related to risk of watershed impairment. The orderings based on these measures provide a first-cut at a consistent nationwide comparison of watersheds with NFS land. Users of the spreadsheets that contain the detailed results of the assessment may alter the weights according to their own understanding of the relative importance of the indicators, producing their own ratings and rankings. Among other things, we find that the non-NFS parts of the watersheds are consistently under much greater stress than the NFS parts, but that the resources at risk are more evenly spread across the NFS and non-NFS parts of the watersheds; and that risk is unevenly spread across the NFS, with most units in the two eastern regions at higher risk than nearly all units in the western regions. The results of this assessment offer a starting point for deciding about risk mitigation efforts, one that could be supplemented by locally available data on additional indicators and by a comparison of the costs and benefits of mitigation options.

Keywords: watershed condition, sediment, nutrients, toxics, national forests

Authors

Thomas C. Brown is an economist with the U.S. Forest Service, Rocky Mountain Research Station.

Pamela Froemke is a GIS analyst with the U.S. Forest Service, Rocky Mountain Research Station.

Preface

This report was produced with two objectives in mind. First, we sought to provide a nationwide assessment based on relatively good quality, consistent data, which could serve as a point of reference for pending decisions about agency watershed condition assessment. Second, we hoped to offer information that would be useful in making broad-scale decisions about where more in-depth assessment would be most helpful. Our end products—this report and its associated spreadsheets of data and metrics of risk to watershed condition—offer a great deal of information about nearly 3700 5th-level watersheds across the lower 48 states. Two qualifications about this information are most important. First, this is a nationwide analysis, which most appropriately supports broad-scale comparisons and decisions. Because good quality nationwide data sets are not available for some variables that may be of interest in specific locations, and because even good quality nationwide data sets sometimes fail to accurately characterize local situations, the results will probably provide only a starting point for watershed assessments at local scales, such as that of a national forest. Also, although we performed the analysis using what for a nationwide assessment is considered a very fine spatial scale, that scale may not be sufficiently fine for local planning needs. Second, because consistent nationwide data on soil quality, on aquatic species populations, and on water quantity, quality, and timing were not available, this assessment examines the *risk* of impaired watershed condition, not the actual condition of watersheds.

Acknowledgments

This study was initiated and partially funded by Strategic Planning and Resource Assessment, Programs and Legislation, U.S. Forest Service, Washington, D.C. The majority of the funding has been provided by the Rocky Mountain Research Station.

The work plan benefited from review and suggestions from Alan Clingenpeel, Mike Furniss, Mark Hudy, Bruce McCammon, John Potyondy, and Kurt Riitters of the Forest Service, and Bruce Jones of the USGS. In addition, we thank Alan Clingenpeel and Mark Hudy for encouragement and numerous hints, techniques, and ideas as we struggled with obtaining and reconciling early versions of the boundaries of 5th-level watersheds and with analyzing broad spatial data sets; Susan Ruzicka of the Forest Service's Automated Lands Project for supplying us with the latest forest ownership data; Raymond Watts of the USGS in Fort Collins for the roads data; Peter Landres of the Leopold Wilderness Research Institute for information about activities in wilderness areas; Ted Geier, Bill Hansen, Sherry Hazelhurst, Suzanne Krieger, David Merritt, Bruce Sims, and Brett Roper of the Forest Service, plus Dave Theobald of Colorado State University, for comments on earlier draft; and Tom Crow, Charlie Luce, and Keith Reynolds of the research branch of the Forest Service and John Potyondy of the Forest Service's Stream Team for comments on a subsequent draft.

Contents

Introduction_____

Although watershed condition is an ongoing concern for the U.S. Forest Service,[1] the agency lacks a systematic nationwide assessment of the condition of its watersheds. The objective of this study was to develop a consistent nationwide assessment of the risk of impaired watershed condition for all watersheds containing National Forest System (NFS) land. The assessment could inform Forest Service decisions on where to focus future, more in-depth watershed assessment,[2] which would in turn help to determine where watershed protection actions would be most effective. The assessment would also provide consistent data for others to use in national or regional watershed analyses of their own. And the assessment would provide an example of what is currently possible in assessing risk of impaired watershed condition at the national scale, which may inform efforts within the agency to develop a process for periodic nationwide watershed assessments.

"Watershed condition" is not a precise term, and means different things to different people. For some, watershed condition refers to the condition of both the soil and the water within the watershed, whereas for others it refers only to those aspects of the watershed affecting the quality, quantity, or timing of the water flowing in or from the watershed. For some, watershed condition includes the habitats of terrestrial plants and animals, even those outside of riparian zones, whereas for others only aquatic and perhaps also riparian biota are of importance. The U.S. Forest Service includes both soil and water functions in its official definition of watershed condition, and in recent practice the agency has also emphasized the importance of ecological conditions throughout the watershed.[3] This assessment of watersheds with NFS land adopts the traditional focus on soil and water conditions.

The national forest preserves were originally set aside for provision of two key resources, water and timber, and for the protection of the watershed functions that supported those resources. Today we would also call those resources "ecosystem goods" and those functions "ecosystem functions." Over time the goals of the national forests have been expanded to the provision of other ecosystem goods including wildlife, range forage, and recreation opportunities. As goals for the national forests have expanded, so also has our understanding of ecosystem functions and the services they provide. Key ecosystem services provided in watersheds include not only water purification and mitigation of floods and droughts, but also soil retention, translocation of nutrients, and maintenance of habitats.[4] An assessment of watershed condition is essentially an assessment of either the current capacity of watersheds to provide ecosystem goods and services, or of the threats to that capacity.

Watersheds of the United States are delineated using a system that divides and subdivides the country into successively smaller basins. At the grossest level there are 20 large basins called "water resource regions" in the United States, each designated by a 2-digit numeric code. Until recently, the finest breakdown for which certified boundaries were available for the entire United States was the 4th-level division, for which there are 2139 hydrologic units, each identified by an 8-digit numeric code (called a hydrologic

---

[1] In recent years the NFS has spent roughly $50 million per year to "maintain and improve watershed conditions."

[2] An example of a more in-depth assessment is the Aquatic and Riparian Effectiveness Monitoring Plan (AREMP) developed as part of the Northwest Forest Plan (Reeves and others, undated). Under this plan, 6th-level watersheds are assessed in three parts: upland area, riparian zone, and stream channel. The small scale allows a detailed assessment that combines onsite inventory with remotely sensed data.

[3] The U.S. Forest Service Manual, chapter 2520, defines watershed condition as "the state of a watershed based upon physical and biological characteristics and processes affecting hydrologic and soil functions." Three condition classes are defined. In class 1 the "physical, chemical, and biologic conditions suggest that soil, aquatic, and riparian systems are predominantly functional in terms of supporting beneficial uses." In classes 2 and 3 those conditions are at risk in being able to, or are unable to, support the beneficial uses, respectively. However, some recent Forest Service descriptions of watershed condition take an even broader view. For example, consider this (dated February 2009) from a Region 8 website: "The ecological significance of ecosystem processes is recognized as essential to good watershed condition. A watershed in good condition has physical structures and biotic resources that support productive ecosystems, the capacity to quickly recover from episodic and chronic disturbances, and conditions that support the natural expression of ecosystem functions and structures (e.g., plant succession, diversity of species and habitats)."

[4] The distinction between goods and services employed here, taken from economic theory, is that goods (in most cases) are tangible, material products (whether or not they are traded in markets), whereas services tend to provide improvements in the condition or location of things of value. Thus, for example, water is a good and water purification a service. Recreation opportunities do not fit neatly into this dichotomy, but typically are treated as goods (Brown and others 2007).

unit code, or HUC).[5] However, even 4th-level units are too large for a useful characterization of watershed condition. Fortunately, certified boundaries for the next finer breakdown, 5th-level hydrologic units, became available for the coterminous United States in early 2009.[6] We base this assessment on 5th-level hydrologic units, which are each identified by a 10-digit HUC and are called "watersheds" herein.

In addition to limiting our effort to watersheds containing NFS land, we further limited the study area to the 48 contiguous states because good quality, comparable data on some variables of interest were not available elsewhere.[7] In the 48 contiguous states there are 18 water resource regions, 2112 4th-level units, and roughly 21,000 5th-level units, of which nearly 3700 have NFS land (table 1).

Our approach in assessing watershed condition emphasizes stressors that tend to impair the condition of watersheds (for example, roads) and resources within the watersheds that are sensitive to such stressors (for example, lakes and reservoirs subject to sedimentation), but not direct measures of watershed condition as indicated by the condition of soil, water, and aquatic organisms. The reason for focusing on stressors and at-risk resources rather than directly on watershed condition variables is not a lack of interest in gauging actual watershed condition; rather it is simply the lack of consistent and readily available nationwide data on soil quality, on water as it leaves the watersheds, and on aquatic populations living in the lakes and streams of the watersheds. It will also be seen that some important stressors (for example, recent severe wildfires) and at-risk resources (for example, presence of pristine fishing stream reaches) are not included in the analysis, again because of the lack of good quality nationwide data sets. We placed a high priority on data quality and consistency across the full set of watersheds. Thus, whereas soil quality and instream measures would allow an assessment of the *result* of watershed impairment, our approach, which focuses on watershed stressors and at-risk resources, can be best characterized as an assessment of the *risk* of watershed impairment.

Table 1. Watersheds and administrative areas analyzed.

NFS region	Number of			Area (km²)		
	Watersheds[a]	NFS units[b]	Wilderness areas[c]	Watershed	NFS	Wilderness
1	494	13	13	238,230	103,424	21,052
2	460	15	46	260,034	87,589	19,005
3	356	11	52	234,535	82,162	10,940
4	624	13	41	315,495	128,167	22,972
5	433	18	56	181,206	82,033	18,281
6	466	17	59	216,591	99,880	18,512
8	489	14	76	239,365	53,645	2,832
9	350	15	50	188,906	48,579	5,356
Total	3672	116	393	1,874,362	685,478	118,949

[a] Watersheds with at least 1% of the area managed by the NFS. Watersheds that span regional boundaries are listed with the region with the greater amount of NFS area within the watershed.

[b] Forest codes were obtained from the Forest Service's Automated Lands Project (ALP) in July 2009. The individual units are listed in the accompanying online material (see footnote 20 for the website address).

[c] Only designated NFS wilderness areas are included. Wilderness areas that span regional boundaries are listed with the region with the greater amount of area within the region.

---

[5] The Water Resources Council, and later the USGS, called these 8-digit basins "cataloguing units" (U.S. Water Resources Council 1978). Recently an inter-agency committee renamed the different levels of hydrologic units, calling 8-digit units "sub-basins" and 10-digit units "watersheds." The inter-agency report is found at: ftp://ftp-fc.sc.egov.usda.gov/NCGC/products/watershed/hu-standards.pdf.

[6] Fifth-level hydrologic units probably provide sufficient detail for a national-level assessment but are generally considered too large for watershed planning at the regional and local scales. At those finer scales, 6th-level (12-digit) units are desired.

[7] Hawaii has no national forests, and although Alaska and Puerto Rico do, data for many variables were lacking there. For example, as of December 2008 we lacked comparable data for Alaska on road density, housing density, drinking water intakes, fire hazard, precipitation, and erosivity.

The inability to assess watershed condition using data on the condition of soils, water, and aquatic organisms highlights an obvious need for improved inventory of soils, lakes, and streams. With data on soil, lake, and stream condition variables, or data on additional stressors and resources at risk, nationwide watershed condition assessments would become more useful. But it must be recognized that there will always be variables of importance in some regional or more local settings that are relatively unimportant in other settings and for which data will therefore be missing in some regions of the country. Budgets will not support collecting all the data we might wish to have. Regional or local analyses, however, allow for more variables and better data. Because of these data and scale issues, assessments at different geographical scales support different kinds of decisions. The limited data available for nationwide assessments support comparisons of broad areas of the country, perhaps aiding in budget allocation among those broad areas, but only approximate the assessments that would be possible at finer scales. Finer-scale analyses using additional, more regionally relevant data along with some first-hand knowledge of field conditions allow enhanced comparison of areas such as watersheds within a NFS unit. And finally, even finer-scale analyses, aided by on-the-ground verification of conditions, allow effective comparison of even smaller areas, such as areas within individual 5th-level watersheds. Finer-scale analysis may, of course, find it useful to lower the spatial scale to 6th-level watersheds.

We provide an ordering of watersheds from lowest to highest level of concern but make no attempt to go to the next step and establish a reference condition against which the watersheds can be compared. A reference condition would, for example, specify the desired minimum state of risk of watershed impairment, allowing us to then separate the watersheds into two groups, those that measure up to the reference condition and those that do not. We forego this logical extension of our analysis for two reasons. First, there

are many possible reference conditions—examples include pre-colonial, pre-industrial, and pre-WW II conditions, as well as the best available current condition within a designated geographic area such as an ecoregion—and the choice of one is a value judgment. Second, even if we chose some basis for specifying a reference condition, precisely characterizing reference conditions for all the various physical and ecological situations across the United States where national forests and grasslands are found would be far beyond our ability. Thus, we restrict our assessment to an ordering of watersheds. Such an ordering places no value judgments on the condition of any one watershed, but it does provide clear relative information, showing, for example, where the watersheds of greatest risk of impairment are found.

This assessment covers only one point in time—or, more precisely, the various recent points in time when the different variables we used were inventoried.[8] An attractive feature of analyses of watershed condition is the possibility of periodic reassessments, thereby allowing measurement of trends in risk of watershed impairment. Indeed, trend analysis is perhaps the most useful role of such an assessment. However, trend analysis requires periodic and consistent data collection for all important variables. This assessment could provide a starting point for nationwide measurement of trends in watershed condition but a less than ideal starting point because of three factors: (1) the variables we used were not all inventoried at the same point in time, thus providing a temporally inconsistent picture of existing (i.e., recent past) watershed conditions; (2) the same variables will be re-inventoried at various times in the future; and (3) the time between inventories may be longer than desired for trend analysis.[9]

The assessment—limited though it is to supporting only broad-scale planning, and relying completely on data sets developed by others—required a great deal of analysis. The assessment involved over 184,500 NFS and non-NFS polygons for which we computed information on over 20 indicators and about 30 background

---

[8] In general, we did not attempt to estimate risk from activities that occurred prior to recent inventories, which may have enhanced the risk of water quality problems, such as agricultural cultivation prior to 2001 when our land use data were amassed. This is not to say that so-called legacy sediment or nutrients are not still impairing water quality; rather, our lack of attention to earlier activities reflects a combination of lack of comparable data and the judgment that earlier activities are less important than more recent activities in characterizing what is currently occurring and what is therefore subject to change. One exception to this general rule, however, is the inclusion of abandoned mines, which may still have important effects on water quality.

[9] A promising possibility is that fine-scale remote sensing data capture and analysis will quickly advance to the point where relevant stressors can be inexpensively monitored on an annual basis.

variables. And the indicators were analyzed at a fine scale—for example, we used a 30 m DEM to calculate slope for isolating steep roads, and a 100 m buffer with the 1:100,000 NHD medium-resolution streams layer to map riparian areas—allowing fairly accurate measures of the indicators, as seen in more detail in the next section.

Methods

We first developed a conceptual framework for characterizing watershed condition and then settled on a procedure for completing the assessment. The procedure has the following five steps:

- Given a consistent set of 5th-level watershed boundaries, delineate NFS and non-NFS polygons within the watersheds.

- Select watershed problems of interest.

- Identify variables relevant to those problems, and obtain geo-referenced data for indicators to characterize those variables.

- Add data for each indicator to the polygon layer, and compute average values of the variables for each polygon.

- Finalize weights, compute scale values, and order the watersheds.

In the following subsections we describe our framework and explain the five steps.

Characterizing Risk of Impaired Watershed Condition

Our underlying goal in characterizing watershed condition was to provide initial information that would eventually help guide watershed management. With this practical goal in mind, the conceptual framework we used to organize our thinking about watershed condition has four basic parts: stressor, problem as indicated by soil and aquatic conditions, affected resources, and mitigating management action (figure 1). A stressor creates or amplifies a problem, which has on-site, down-slope, downstream, or downwind impacts on resources. Management actions can affect the stressor and thereby lessen the impact of the problem.

To illustrate the conceptual framework, consider a common problem in forested watersheds: sediment in streams (figure 1). Excess sediment in streams has various deleterious effects, including damage to aquatic life, sedimentation of reservoirs, and increased costs of treating water for municipal use. Existence of a problem is indicated in measurements of soil and instream conditions or revealed in damage to resources at risk. Potential causes of this problem (i.e., stressors) include vehicle use on unpaved roads and skid trails, severe wildfire, and excessive livestock grazing in sensitive areas. Potential actions, or management options, available to land managers fall into three groups: road and trail management, forest fuels and vegetation management, and riparian area management. Specific management actions include constraints on OHV use, waterbars for skid trails, prescribed burning so as to avoid potentially more destructive wildfire, and livestock management including fencing of riparian areas.[10]

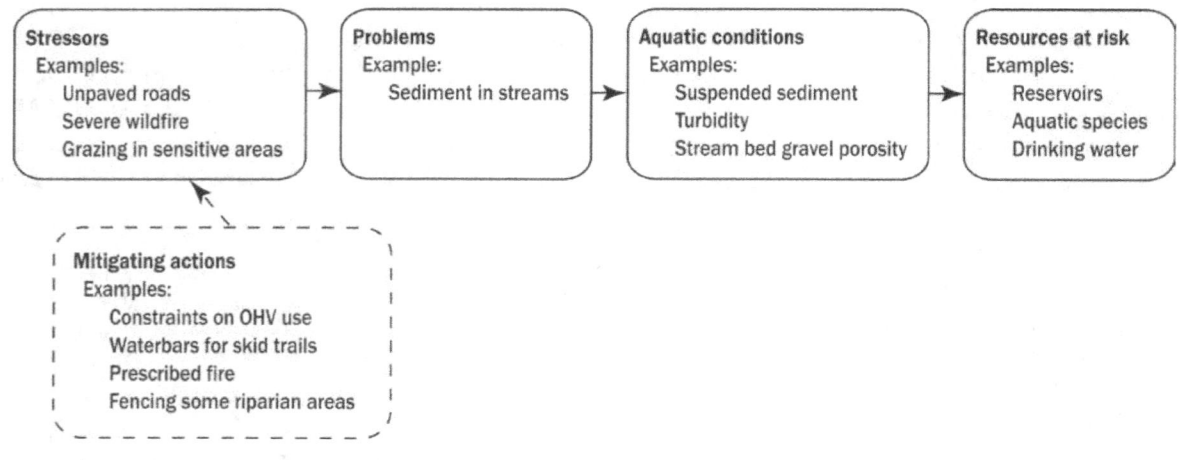

Figure 1. Conceptual framework.

Given the practical objective of this effort, characterizations of watershed condition must reflect an identified problem affected by at least one identified stressor, and there must be at least one possible action that could mitigate the impacts by affecting the stressor. Problems without identifiable stressors, and problems that are not amenable to mitigation via management action, are not of primary interest. That said, in this effort we are not concerned with *which* management action should be taken. Our focus is on obtaining an initial estimate of the degree to which causes of identified problems amenable to mitigation are present. This focus on individual problems amenable to mitigation is different from most prior assessments of watershed condition. Prior assessments (Clingenpeel 2003; Jones and others 1997; U.S. Forest Service 2000a, 2000b) have typically produced general watershed characterizations or rankings that give users an overall idea of the condition of the assessed watersheds, not information about individual problems.

Our conceptual framework emphasizes human-caused stressors. Purely natural levels of soil movement, nutrient leaching, or other natural processes—although sometimes undesirable—are not of primary interest because avoiding natural stressors is generally not an option. Within this framework, wildfire is a special case, for although wildfire is a natural phenomenon, the severity of wildfire has been enhanced by past management actions in many forests with short fire recurrence intervals. For this reason, potentially damaging wildfire is included as a stressor. In addition, to the extent that natural processes exacerbate the effect of human actions—as high erosion potential exacerbates the deleterious effect of road construction—they too are of interest. For example, we include stressors for cultivation on highly erosive soils and roads on steep slopes.

Primarily we are concerned with stressors involving human actions that occur on the watershed at issue. This is both because actions that could stress a watershed often occur on that watershed, and because a local link of cause to effect increases the likelihood that the action causing the stress will be addressed. However, one important exception to this general rule is atmospheric deposition, which is an important cause of stress for some watersheds and almost always results from actions (for example, burning of fossil fuels at power plants) off of the watershed.

Delineating Areas of Consideration

For this assessment we used the 5th-level watershed boundaries provided by the Natural Resources Conservation Service (NRCS) and NFS boundaries from the Forest Service's Automated Lands Project (ALP). The full set of 5th-level watershed boundaries for the contiguous 48 states became available in March 2009. The ALP boundaries were obtained in July of 2009 (figure 2).

Figure 2. NFS parcels, also showing region numbers and boundaries.

---

[10] This simple model is not limited to watershed applications. For example, a person may be stressed by overwork, poor nutrition, and a sedentary life style, leading to problems such as hardening of the arteries or diabetes, which may be indicated by measurements of the body's condition such as of blood pressure and blood chemistry, and which manifest in effects on resources at risk such as disposable income (based on the logic that increases in health care expenses reduce disposable income) or one's ability to enjoy outdoor activities.

Figure 3. 3672 5th-level watersheds with at least 1% NFS land, also showing NFS region numbers and boundaries.

Following watershed boundary delineation, we eliminated from consideration all watersheds with less than 1 percent NFS land, for two reasons. First, when very little of a watershed is in NFS land, management on that land can have little impact on overall conditions within the watershed. Second, when only a small amount of NFS land is being analyzed, any errors in the data on the indicator variables may overly influence the characterization of that watershed and the ranking of the watersheds. Applying our 1 percent rule resulted in a total of 3672 watersheds (figure 3).

Within each watershed we distinguished between NFS land and non-NFS land. Any land not designated as NFS was considered non-NFS land. In addition, within NFS land we distinguish between designated wilderness areas and other NFS land, again using ALP boundary data. Thus, each watershed contains up to three categories of land, with some containing only one or two categories. [11]

The 3672 watersheds range in size from 27 to 1652 km^2 and have a median area of 474 km^2, with 81 percent being from 200 to 800 km^2 in size (figure 4). The NFS regions contain from 350 to 624 watersheds each, from 11 to 18 NFS units, and from 13 to 76 wilderness areas (table 1). Across the regions (as may be computed from data in table 1), the average watershed size varies from 418 km^2 in Region 5 to 659 km^2 in Region 3; the average NFS unit size varies from 10,067 km^2 in Region 5 to 24,269 km^2 in Region 4; and the average wilderness area size varies from 37 km^2 in Region 8 to 1460 km^2 in Region 1. Thus, the regions vary relatively little in typical watershed size but greatly in unit and wilderness area size.

Figure 5 shows the area in each region that is NFS wilderness, other NFS land, and non-NFS land. Across all of the watersheds, 63 percent is non-NFS of which 23 percent is other federal land, and 37 percent is in the NFS of which 17 percent is designated wilderness.

Identified Problems

There are many soil- and water-related watershed problems that could be studied, including sediment and nutrients in lakes and streams; dissolved metals and other toxic chemicals (which together we will call toxics) in lakes, streams, and soils; alteration of stream temperature;[12] diminished water flows; pathogens in lakes and streams; invasive aquatic

---

[11] When delineating these land categories within a watershed, isolated slivers of land often appeared along boundaries, which may occur by chance or because of errors or inconsistencies in boundary delineation. For example, a national forest boundary may proceed along a ridge line at the edge of a watershed but may not match the watershed boundary exactly, leaving isolated narrow strips of non-NFS land along the boundary. In an attempt to remove erroneous or trivially small parcels, we eliminated a polygon if the total area of the polygon parcel within the watershed had a ratio of area (in m^2) to perimeter (in m) $\leq$ 100 (a smaller criterion of 50 was used for the Superior National Forest because of the preponderance of small private parcels within the national forest). Using these rules, we eliminated 1220 slivers.

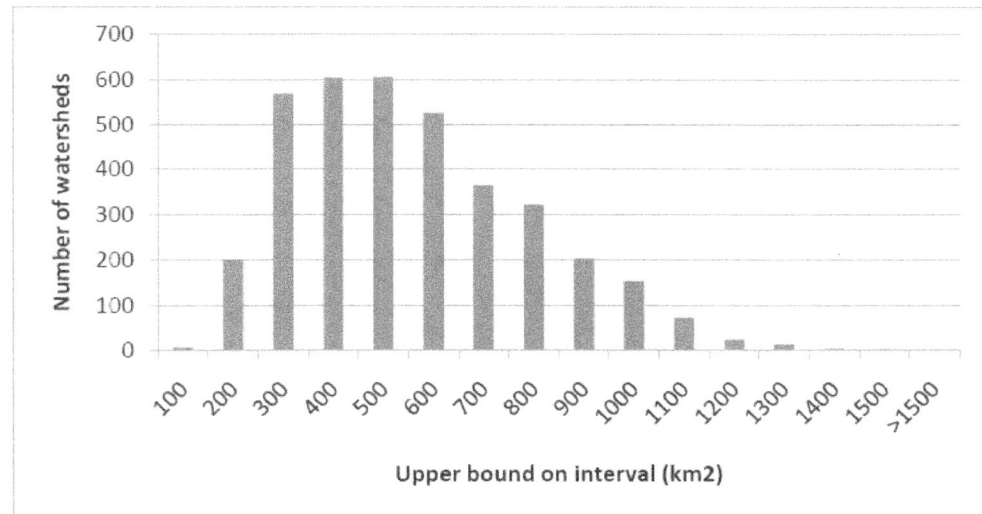

Figure 4. Size distribution of the 3672 watersheds.

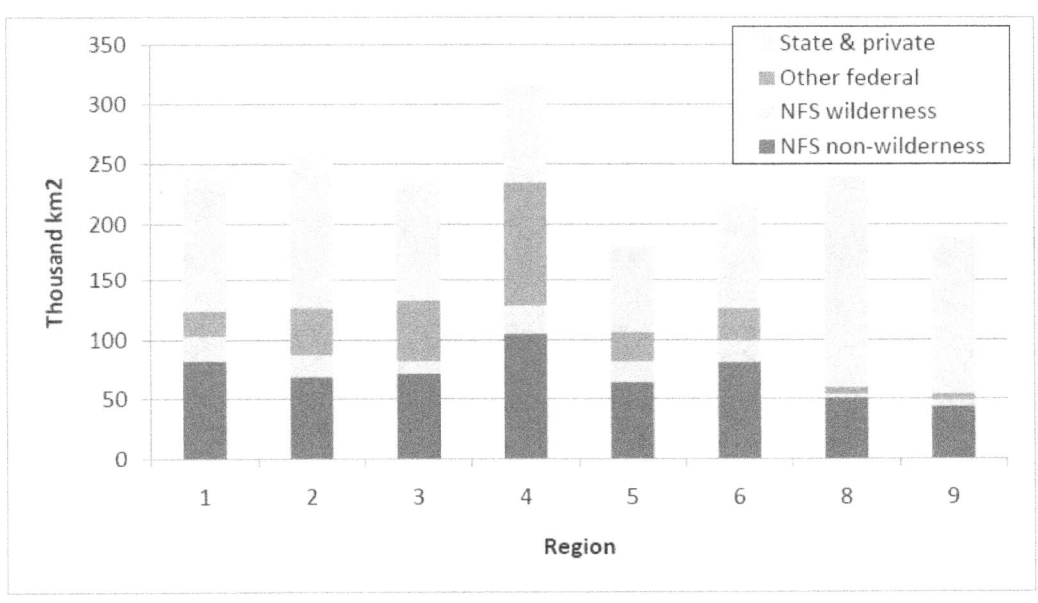

Figure 5. Watershed area by region.

species; soil compaction; stream channel modification; and loss of hydrologic connectivity. Lacking good quality nationwide data sets for variables relevant to some of these problems, we limited our effort to three problems—sediments, nutrients, and toxics—all of which can end up in lakes and streams and some of which can harm soils, thereby damaging valuable resources (table 2). These three problems capture four of the five most frequently cited causes of fresh water impairment.[13]

---

[12] Stream temperature is a major issue in some forest areas, such as in the Pacific Northwest. Because alteration of stream temperature occurs primarily via removal of riparian vegetation, stream temperature is largely a riparian area issue, not a watershed-wide issue. In any case, obtaining good nationwide data on riparian vegetation density and water temperature at the 5th-level watershed scale is problematic.

[13] In November 2007 the EPA (http://oaspub.epa.gov/waters/national_rept.control) listed 36 possible causes of impaired waters on which states report pursuant to section 303(d) of the Clean Water Act. The five most frequently cited causes, in order of declining frequency, are mercury, pathogens, sediment, metals other than mercury, and nutrients.

Table 2. Variables for assessing watershed condition and potential indicators.

Variable	Potential indicator
Stressor	
Human presence	Population density
	Rate of population increase
	Housing density
	Urban land cover
	Housing in riparian areas
Industry	Number of industrial sites
Roads	Road density
	Road-stream crossings
	Roads in riparian areas
	Roads on steep slopes
	OHV use levels
Agriculture	Cultivation on gentle slopes
	Cultivation on steep slopes
	Cultivation on highly erosive soils
	Cultivation in riparian areas
Timber harvest	Recent harvest
Mining	Number of mines (active and inactive)
Livestock and poultry	Animal density
Feedlots	Number of feedlots
Atmospheric deposition	Precipitation chemistry data (e.g., SO_4^{2-}, NO_3^-, Hg deposition)
Dams	Number of dams
Natural processes	
Wildfire	Recent severe burns
	Area of potentially damaging wildfire
Precipitation	Erosivity
Erosion	RUSLE estimates or erosive soil coverage
Landslides	Susceptibility to landslides
At-risk resource	
Water bodies and stream segments	Lakes and reservoirs
	Pristine streams
	Recreational fishing visitor days
	Designated wild and scenic rivers
Drinking water supply	Municipal water intakes
Animal and plant species	Aquatic animal and plant T&E species
	Terrestrial animal and plant T&E species
Stream and soil condition	
Water quality	Average concentration of selected constituents
	Recent listing of impaired streams and water bodies from the EPA's 303(d) TMDS tracking system
Water temperature	Average temperature readings at all available USGS stations in watershed
Water quantity	Recent mean annual flow as a percent of pre-settlement mean annual flow
Fish populations	Fish population by species, compared with unimpaired potential
Soil quality	Measures of key constituents and indicators

USDA Forest Service RMRS-GTR-251. 2010.

Selecting Indicators

Three groups of variables were identified as useful for the conceptual framework outlined above: stressors, at-risk resources, and watershed condition variables (left-hand column of table 2). *Stressors* are either human activities or influences, such as mining, that may place stress on the watershed and that, being human influences, are amenable to change via human action; or natural events or susceptibilities that may intersect with human activities, such as wildfire or soil erosion. *At-risk resources* are human uses and concerns that are vulnerable to stressors. Examples include reservoirs that are susceptible to sedimentation, pristine streams subject to deterioration, and endangered species whose habitat may be harmed. Finally, *condition* variables are instream or soil measures indicating whether or not a problem exists, such as measures of water quality.

The variables of each group are represented by a set of indicators, which together characterize watershed condition according to our conceptual model. As explained below, we first identified a set of potential indicators for each group of variables (table 2), and then selected a subset of those indicators for which good quality, spatially consistent data were available.

Stressors

The largest, most complex set of indicators in the conceptual model is associated with watershed stressors. Each identified problem—sediment, nutrients, and toxics—provides a context and rationale for an associated set of stressors as discussed below. Notice that the importance of some stressors depends on where the activity occurs. For example, the effect of agricultural cultivation is most serious when it occurs on steeper slopes, and OHV use is more serious when it occurs on highly erosive soils or near streams. Thus several of the stressor variables are specific to slopes, soils, or hydrologic networks within a watershed.

Sediments consist of soil particles that are carried along in stream flow, some of which settle on the stream bottom or in lakes and reservoirs. Suspended sediments increase turbidity and transport plant nutrients, toxics, pathogens, and other potential pollutants attached to the soil particles. Sustained high turbidity can reduce photosynthesis by algae, reduce the success of sight-feeding fish, and degrade the quality of drinking water (or increase the cost of water treatment). Settling particles reduce the porosity of gravel beds, causing anaerobic conditions unsuitable for spawning and blocking emergence of fry from the gravels, lower storage capacity of lakes and reservoirs, and interfere with navigation.

Based on 1982 NRI (National Resource Inventory) estimates of erosion on nonfederal rural lands, in light of sediment transport and delivery predictions, discharge rates into rivers and streams from cropland were estimated to be more than five times the rate from forest land (Gianessi and others 1986). Of the total sediment discharge from non-federal lands, 57 percent was estimated to originate on cropland, 16 percent on rangeland, 10 percent on forest land, 5 percent on pastures, and 12 percent on other lands (mines, quarries, farmsteads, and other uses). Given the relative amounts of land of these different land covers, cropland and other lands are clearly the land covers of greatest concern. Jones and others (2001) found that stream suspended sediment loads across the United States were positively associated with the percent of the watershed in urban cover and negatively associated with wetland and riparian forest covers. In addition to activities associated with the land covers of concern (plowing and other soil disturbances with agriculture, construction in urban areas, and mining), several other activities are recognized as important causes of suspended sediment. Perhaps the most important of these is road construction, which both exposes soil surfaces and concentrates surface runoff, thereby increasing sediment transport capacity (Forman and Alexander 1998). These effects were found to increase with slope and with loss of vegetation on the cutslope and in roadside ditches (Luce and Black 1999).

For forest management activities, Binkley and Brown (1993) concluded based on a review of many empirical studies that concentrations of suspended sediment often increase after management activities such as road construction, timber harvest, and forest site preparation following harvest, but that effects are highly variable across soils and slopes. Severe forest fires (for example, Benavides-Solorio and MacDonald 2001; Cannon and others 2001; Moody and Martin 2001; Neary and others 2005) and livestock grazing, especially in riparian areas (for example, Johnson and others 1978; Kauffman and Krueger 1984; Wohl and Carline 1996), can also add to suspended sediment. The impact of severe wildfire on sediment movement depends critically on the timing of precipitation events. Heavy rain following the Buffalo Creek (Moody and Martin 2001) and Hayman (Graham 2003) fires along the Colorado Front Range provided vivid examples of the potential for erosion following wildfire.

Livestock grazing is an important cause of soil disturbance and related suspended sediment, especially in arid environments, where water is a limiting factor and grazing animals naturally congregate near streams and other water bodies (Bartley and others 2010). In rangeland environments, where crop agriculture and other land use activities are less common, most of the damage to streams and riparian systems is thought to result from livestock grazing (Belsky and others 1999).

Based on this evidence, we propose that increases in suspended sediment will be associated with the following stressors: urban and suburban land uses including building construction; agriculture; mines, quarries, gravel pits, and other such concentrated rural land disturbances; roads, especially in riparian areas; timber harvest; livestock grazing, especially near streams; and severe wildfire (table 2). These activities tend to cause more erosion if they occur on steeper slopes, on highly erosive soils, and in areas of high erosivity (i.e., high precipitation volume and intensity).

Nutrients, primarily forms of nitrogen and phosphorous, are essential for primary food production in aquatic ecosystems, but at high levels they can cause excessive growth of aquatic plants and animals, which in turn cause murky water, algal blooms, and dense mats of aquatic plants, all characteristics of eutrophication. The U.S. Environmental Protection Agency (1990) concluded that eutrophication was the most common impairment of surface waters in the United States. Background levels of nutrients tend to be low for natural land covers not subject to atmospheric nitrogen deposition, but land uses and atmospheric deposition can cause levels to rise much above those background levels (Mueller and Helsel 1996).[14]

Nonpoint source discharges of nutrients are estimated to be over five times as great as point source discharges (Carpenter and others 1998). In a nationwide analysis, Omernik (1977) found that annual nutrient concentrations in streams draining predominantly agricultural watersheds were about nine times higher than in streams draining predominantly forested watersheds, and about four times higher than in streams draining predominantly rangeland watersheds. Smith and others (1987) reported that changes in agricultural fertilizer use and atmospheric deposition accounted for the significant increases in nitrogen concentrations across the United States observed over the period 1974 to 1981. Similarly, Driscoll and others (2003) found that the main anthropogenic nitrogen inputs to Northeastern watersheds were from atmospheric deposition, agriculture, and human food importation and consumption (and related sewage). Jones and others (2001) found for the Chesapeake Bay Basin that high nutrient levels were associated mainly with agricultural and urban land covers and with atmospheric deposition of nitrogen. Carpenter and others (1998) and Wickham and others (2005) both concluded that nitrogen and phosphorous concentrations across the United States were largely associated with agricultural and urban land uses. Concentrated animal feeding operations (feedlots) are also a significant source of nutrients (Mallin 2000). Conversely, forest cover, especially in riparian areas, was negatively associated with stream nutrient levels (Jones and others 2001) and timber harvest tends to have only a small impact on stream nutrient levels (Binkley and Brown 1993). Based on all this evidence, we propose that the following stressors are important for stream nutrients: human presence indicated by urban land cover and housing density (the latter will pick up rural as well as urban inputs), agriculture, feedlots, and atmospheric deposition (table 2).[15]

Toxics are chemicals that cause damage to plants and animals (both vertebrates and invertebrates, and including humans) at low levels. They include toxic heavy metals (for example, mercury, lead, cadmium, and arsenic), some pesticides (including herbicides), some industrial chemicals (for example, PCBs), some pharmaceuticals, and acids. Heavy metals exist naturally and are essential for life but are toxic at elevated levels. Mining can greatly increase heavy

---

[14] Chronically elevated nitrogen levels in soils can also inhibit growth of alpine and subalpine plant species, including evergreen forests, and continual acid deposition can increase rates of nutrient leaching from the soil profile (Driscoll and others 2003). However, in most locations nitrogen is a limiting factor and nitrogen from atmospheric deposition acts as a fertilizer.

[15] Most atmospheric deposition results from activities over which watershed managers have no control. Atmospheric deposition is included here nevertheless because such deposition can exacerbate the nutrient problem, making land-based mitigation all the more important.

metal discharge, and long-abandoned mining sites may continue to contribute excess levels of such metals to the stream as metal-bearing fine sediments are washed out of tailings by heavy rains or enter the surface water from polluted shallow groundwater near the mines (for example, Courtney and Clements 2002; Roline 1988; Rosner 1998). Of course, the pollution potential of mines differs greatly with the geology of the area (and thus the substances mined) and the mining processes used. Other sources of toxic levels of heavy metals are some activities, such as some manufacturing and refining processes, common in urban areas (for example, Kelly and others 1996; Pouyat and others 1995), vehicle traffic (for example, Albasel and Cottenie 1985; Forman and Alexander 1998), and thermo-electric power plant emissions.[16] Pesticides are used primarily on agricultural lands and in urban and suburban areas. Pesticide application rates (kg/km²/yr) on agricultural land tend to be roughly 1000 times greater than rates on forested land (Brown and Binkley 1994). Although uses of herbicides in urban areas do not approach those in agriculture, uses of insecticides have been found to be similar (for example, Hoffman and others 2000; Paul and Meyer 2001). Industrial chemicals tend, of course, to be used at industrial and mining sites. Pharmaceuticals are mainly associated with the presence of humans or domesticated animals. Acids (primarily sulfuric and nitric acid) reach the soil or water bodies in acidic precipitation resulting from the burning of fossil fuels (for example, at power plants, in vehicles). These acids can damage leaves and needles and lower the pH of water bodies into which they fall. Further, when washed into the soil, the acids, if not buffered sufficiently, can leach soil nutrients and toxic substances from the soil, hampering plant growth and, when washed on to receiving waters, aquatic life as well (Driscoll and others 2003). Based on this evidence, we suggest that the following stressors are relevant to toxics: mining of heavy metals and other toxic substances; agriculture; activities associated with housing, landscape maintenance, and commercial enterprise; industrial sites; feedlots; and atmospheric deposition of acids and heavy metals (table 2).

Resources at risk

Resources at risk of damage from the stressors just mentioned include (1) water bodies (mainly lakes, reservoirs, and marshes), which may support a variety of uses including water storage, recreation, scenic viewing, species habitat, and water supply for various uses, and which are subject to damage from sedimentation or water quality degradation; (2) stream segments that support one or more of a variety of uses including species habitat, preservation goals (perhaps as part of the Wild and Scenic River system), recreation (including fishing, swimming, boating, hiking, and picnicking), water supply, and navigation, all of which are subject to the three aforementioned watershed problems; (3) drinking water intakes; and (4) sensitive animal and plant species (table 2). For each resource at risk, one ideally would measure a trend, the rate of change in the quantity or quality of the resource, such as the sedimentation rate of reservoirs, the gain or loss in length of pristine streams, the change in the quality of water at drinking water intakes, or the rate at which threatened and endangered (T&E) species are listed or delisted. Lacking data to support measurement of trends, one could merely identify the presence of such resources at risk, such as the area of lakes, length of pristine streams, or number of T&E species.

Measures of watershed condition

The condition of soils, streams, lakes, and reservoirs is indicated by measures of soil quality and productivity and of water quantity (volume and timing), quality, and temperature as well as measures of aquatic species populations (table 2). Of course there are many water quality constituents and many aquatic species that may be of interest.

Indicators

To assess watershed condition, variables must be represented by measurable indicators. For example, the roads stressor might be represented by a measure of road density such as kilometers of road per square kilometer of watershed, and general human presence might be represented by population density, rate of

---

[16] Power plants affect mercury in watersheds in two ways. First, mercury is a direct by-product of coal burning (roughly one-half of the electricity produced in the U.S. is from coal-fired plants). Mercury and other substances from coal burning reach land downwind in wet or dry deposition. Second, acidic atmospheric deposition—which forms when emissions of SO_2 and nitrogen oxides (NO_2, NO) convert to acids when they come in contact with water in the atmosphere—may dissolve mercury and other toxic elements (e.g., aluminum) in the soil, which then may be taken up by plants or leached from the soil and flow on to rivers, lakes, and estuaries.

population change, or housing density. Table 2 lists many of the indicators that were considered for representing the identified variables.

The indicators in table 2 are listed without consideration of data availability. Table 3 lists the indicators that we ultimately chose to characterize risk of one or more problems, along with their associated spatial data sets and the methods we used to compute the indicator variables. Selection of indicators was constrained by the availability of good quality, comprehensive data.

Table 4 lists indicators we did not use along with the reason for exclusion, which in most cases was the lack of comprehensive and consistent data.[17] Unfortunately, and most importantly, we did not find or obtain adequate data on several important stressors (for example, recent fires, recent timber harvests, feedlots, OHV use levels), some key resources at risk (for example, important streams, presence of native fish populations), or any stream or soil condition variables.

Table 5 lists background variables that are used to describe the watersheds, but are not themselves indicators used to order watersheds. These variables include purely descriptive measures (for example, watershed mean precipitation rate and mean elevation), variables used in the computation of indicators (for example, watershed population, total length of streams in the watershed), and miscellaneous other variables (for example, length of impaired streams as listed in the EPA TMDS tracking system).

The stressors fall into five groups (table 3). For example, human population density and growth, housing density, and percent urban land cover fall within the development group. Indicators within a group may be significantly correlated. Yet each may make a unique contribution to the problem at hand, as does housing density in capturing the location of sources of nutrients from second homes that are not reflected in population data. We attempt to control for

---

[17] Hudy and others (2008) use four criteria for selecting independent variables: completeness, range, redundancy, and responsiveness to the dependent variable. Because we lack a quantitative dependent variable, we could not gauge responsiveness. Completeness refers to comprehensive and consistent data, a criterion on which we placed considerable emphasis. Range refers to the ability of the variable to distinguish among watersheds; the ranges we observed were sufficient that we did not eliminate any variables on this basis. Redundancy is measured by the correlations among prospective dependent variables. We deal with redundancy via our weighting procedure.

Table 3. Approach to indicator measurement.[a]

Indicator	Approach
Stressors by group	
Development group	
Population density	Area-weighted population per km2 from 2000 census tract data.
Population growth	Percent increase in area-weighted density per km2 from year 1990 to year 2000 using county census data (census tract boundaries changed from 1990 to 2000).
Developed land cover	Percent of watershed in developed land cover (classes 21, 22, 23, and 24) from 2001 300m National Land Cover Dataset (NLCD) data, released by the U.S. Geological Survey.
Housing density	Housing units per km^2 in year 2000 based on 2000 US Census Bureau block (SF1) datasets, from Dave Theobald's 100 m2 / cell data set.[b]
Roads group	
Road density	Meters of road (paved & unpaved together) per km^2 of watershed land (excluding water bodies) based on the 2000 Geographic Data Technologies (GDT) roads database.[c]
Road-stream crossings	Number of road-stream crossings per km of stream, from GDT roads intersected with the USGS 2004 National Hydrography Dataset (NHD) medium-resolution (1-to-100,000) stream coverage.[d]
Roads in riparian areas	Total road length in meters (m) within riparian areas per km^2 of riparian area (riparian area defined as 100m each side of stream), using GDT roads and medium-resolution NHD stream coverage.[e]
Roads on steep slopes	Total length of roads (km) in areas with slope >45% per km^2 of watershed, based on GDT roads and 30m, 1 degree DEM (1998). Potentially weighted by erosivity.

Table 3. *Continued.*

Indicator	Approach
Stressors by group	
Farm and ranch group	
Cultivation on gentle slopes	Percent of watershed area in agricultural land cover (i.e., cultivation) on slopes ≤ 3% (Jones and others 2000; Wischmeier and Smith 1978). Cultivation from 300m 2001 NLCD. Cultivated area defined as NLCD classes 81 (pasture and hay) and 82 (cultivated crops). Slopes based on 300m, 1 degree DEM (1998). Potentially weighted by erosivity.
Cultivation on steep slopes	Percent of watershed area in cultivation on slopes > 3%; same sources as cultivation on gentle slopes. Potentially weighted by erosivity.
Cultivation—all slopes	Percent of watershed in cultivation; same source as cultivation on gentle slopes.
Cultivation on highly erosive soils	Percent of watershed area in cultivation on erosive soils, with erosive soils specified from the 1998 BASINS STATSGO data, where erosive soils are those with K factor times the square root of maximum slope range exceeding a threshold of 1.64; cultivated area determined as described above. Potentially weighted by erosivity.
Livestock grazing	Animal units per km^2 in year 2007 based on USDA Census of Agriculture county data, released by the National Agricultural Statistics Service.[f]
Confined animal feeding	Animal units per km^2 in year 2007 based on USDA Census of Agriculture county data, released by the National Agricultural Statistics Service.[g]
Mining group	
Mining land cover	Percent of watershed in mining land cover (class 32, quarries, mines, gravel pits) from 1994 300m NLCD data.[h]
Mines	Total number of active and inactive mine sites potentially yielding toxics per 1000 km^2 of watershed, from the 1998 US Bureau of Mines MAS/MILS database.[i,j]
Other group	
Area of potentially damaging wildfire	Percent of area with high risk of losing key ecosystem components in a fire, from the 1 km grid Fire Regime Current Condition Classes (Schmidt and others 2000), condition class 3 ("fire regimes have been significantly altered from their historical range; the risk of losing key ecosystem components is high").[k]
Atmospheric deposition—acid forming compounds	Mean annual (2000-2006) input of NO_3^- and SO_4^{2-} in kg/ha, in wet atmospheric deposition from the National Atmospheric Deposition Program data.[l]
Dams	Number of dams per km^2 of watershed, from the 2009 version of the National Inventory of Dams (NID) database maintained by the Army Corps of Engineers.[m]
At-risk resources	
Water bodies (lakes, reservoirs, etc.)	Presence of water bodies (m of water body perimeter per km^2 of watershed) based on the medium-resolution NHD water bodies data released by the USGS in 1999.[n] In the NHD, water bodies include lakes, ponds, reservoirs, playas, swamps, marshes, and ice masses; we excluded playas and ice masses for this indicator.
Municipal water intakes	Total number of intakes per km^2 of watershed, from the 2009 EPA's Safe Drinking Water Information System, Federal Version.
Wild and scenic rivers	Length (m) of wild and scenic rivers per km^2 of watershed, with length from the data set Federal Land Features of the United States—Parkways and Scenic Rivers (1:2,000,000), of the National Atlas of the United States, 2006, originally extracted from USGS digital line graph data.
T&E aquatic species	Number of aquatic animal and plant species with an ESA status of threatened or endangered, from the NatureServe database.[o,p]
T&E terrestrial species	Number of terrestrial animal and plant species with an ESA status of threatened or endangered that are not also aquatic species, from the NatureServe database.[o,q]

[a] This approach is applied to entire watersheds, to NFS land within the watersheds, and to non-NFS land within the watersheds (where "watershed" is used in this table, the designation may refer to either whole watersheds or each of these two portions of watersheds).

[b] The data are reported in 15 classes, with each class representing a range in units per 1000 hectares. For example, class 2 is 2–8 units/1000 ha and class 10 is 248–494 units/1000 ha. The smallest (1st) and largest (15th) classes are unbounded, at <= 1 and >24,711 units/1000 ha, respectively. We converted classes to numbers of units per thousand hectares by using the midpoint of the range of each class (for the 1st and 15th classes we assigned 0.5 and 30,000 units/1000 ha), and computed the average density across the cells within an area of interest.

[c] The GDT roads coverage is an offspring of TIGER, which was assembled in the late 1980s from a variety of source materials that reflected quad mapping over many years. Thus, the GDT roads coverage is both generally out-of-date and inconsistent across space in terms of when the roads were inventoried. However, roads are such an important variable that a road coverage is essential for watershed condition assessment. The GDT road coverage is considered sufficiently precise to support only broad-scale comparisons.

[d] The NHD stream coverage is based on topographic contour maps, which generally do not include all streams. For example, in one careful comparison, Hansen (2001) found for a 728 km^2 watershed in the Southeast that the 1-to-100,000 NHD coverage captured only about one-half of the total perennial stream length (the 1-to-24,000 coverage captured about three-fourths of perennial stream length). Further, almost none of the intermittent and ephemeral streams were captured by the NHD coverage. Hansen's findings may not apply to other regions of the U.S. We examined the 2009 NHD as a replacement for the 2004 NHD, but at the time we tested it the newer version had many missing records and was therefore not used.

[e] Using a 200m buffer around all streams is a simplification that fails to reflect how the actual size of riparian areas varies across different topography. In mountainous terrain the riparian area may be much narrower than 200m, whereas on flat land where streams are poorly differentiated the riparian area may be much wider.

[f] The following livestock categories were included (listed here with the Ag Census tables from which the data came): cattle (table 11); horses (table 15); sheep (table 16); goats (table 17); llamas, alpacas, bison, deer, elk, and mules (table 24). Animal unit computations were based on the following conversion factors: cattle (1), horses (1.25); sheep (0.2); goats (0.2); llamas (0.2), alpacas (0.2), bison (1.25), deer (0.2), elk (0.5), and mules (0.8). Animals were assumed to be found only on slopes of less than 30%. The grazing density on forest land was assumed to be 0.4 times the density on other lands. Only cattle, horses, and sheep were assumed to be found on NFS land, whereas all listed species were potentially found on non-NFS land. The following animal species were assumed to occur only on the following cover classes: cattle, horses, and sheep on forest (classes 41, 42, and 43); all species on range (classes 52 and 71) and on agriculture pasture (class 81); cattle, sheep, goats, llamas, and alpacas on agriculture crop land (class 82); and horses, mules, alpacas, and llamas on low-density developed land (classes 21 and 22 only). Within available land areas, animals were assumed to be spread evenly across the area. The density for a watershed or part of a watershed was computed as an area-weighted average of respective county-level densities.

[g] The following livestock and poultry categories were included (listed here with the Ag Census tables from which the data came): fed cattle (table 11); hogs (table 12); chickens (layers, pullets, broilers, table 13); turkeys (table 13); mink (table 22); rabbits (table 24). Animal unit computations were based on the following conversion factors: fed cattle (1); hogs (0.3); chickens (0.003); turkeys (0.015); mink (0.01); and rabbits (0.01). Operations were restricted to slopes of less than 30%, and to non-NFS land. Fed cattle was assumed to occur only on range (classes 52 and 71) and agricultural lands (classes 81 and 82); hogs, chickens, turkey, and mink were assumed to occur only on agricultural lands (classes 81 and 82); rabbits were assumed to occur only on agricultural lands (classes 81 and 82) and low-density developed land (classes 21 and 22). Within available land areas, animals were assumed to be spread evenly across the area. The density for a watershed or part of a watershed was computed as an area-weighted average of respective county-level densities.

[h] The 2001 NLCD includes quarries, mines, and gravel pits within the barren land class, which also includes bedrock, desert pavement, scarps, talus, volcanic material, and sand dunes. We used the earlier (1992) NLCD for this stressor because it isolated mining impacts.

[i] The MAS/MILS data set relies in part on state-level data collection efforts that sometimes differed in methods, resulting in inconsistencies across states (Shields and others 1995). The data set was included here nonetheless because of the importance of mining to water quality. We removed what were, for our purposes, duplicate records by dissolving on SEQNUM and filtered using "bad" mines criteria.

[j] To select toxic commodities we relied on the draft unpublished report "Guidance for Implementation of Trace Elements National Synthesis Within the National Water-Quality Assessment Program," table 2b (Trace Elements of Interest to the National Water-Quality Assessment Program—Water), produced by the Trace Elements National Synthesis Planning Team, USGS, 1998 (226 pages). A mine was included if it produced at least one of the following commodities: aluminum, antimony, arsenic, barium, beryllium, boron, chromium, coal, cobalt, copper, gold, iron, lead, manganese, mercury, molybdenum, nickel, silver, sulfur, titanium, uranium, vanadium, or zinc.

[k] An option, not employed herein, is to weight the wildfire stressor by erosivity.

[l] The National Atmospheric Deposition Program data we used were in the form of a nationwide spatially interpolated grid at the 2.5 km level of resolution available at http://NADP.sws.uiuc.edu.

[m] This stressor was not actually used (i.e., it was assigned zero weight) because dams do not directly cause the selected problems. It is included here nonetheless because it is such a significant stressor for other problems and is available in RWI.xls if users would like to assign it a positive weight in their own analyses.

[n] This indicator is intended to capture the potential vulnerability of water quality of standing water bodies to activities on the land. Perimeter was used instead of area because perimeter was thought to better reflect the connectivity of water bodies to the surrounding land. The correlation of perimeter to area across all water bodies in the full set of watersheds is 0.86.

[o] This indicator uses NatureServe's Element Occurrence species location database. The data we obtained track species with federal status assigned pursuant to the Endangered Species Act, including not only listed threatened and listed endangered (T&E) species but also species proposed for listing or species that are candidates for listing. This indicator, however, includes only listed endangered and listed threatened species (plants and animals together). A species was assigned a habitat value by NatureServe if the habitat is known to contribute significantly to the survival or reproduction of the species at some point in its live cycle. Thus, some species were assigned to both aquatic and terrestrial habitats (double-counting of species occurred in 802 watersheds). Information on non-listed species and listed species not yet assigned habitat values is presented in table B1. Species' geographical ranges are imprecisely mapped. Mapping accuracy is categorized in the NatureServe data as high, medium, or low. We used rules for accepting a species as present in the watershed that differed by accuracy class, as explained in Appendix B.

[p] The aquatic indicator includes species assigned aquatic habitat values. Some T&E species have not yet been assigned the habitat values necessary to label them as being either aquatic or terrestrial; unlabeled species occurrences account for 2.6% of all listed species occurrences (and 3% of all non-listed species occurrences). The number of aquatic T&E species includes the subset of aquatic "obligate" species, those species that spend their lives in water, including crayfishes, fairy, clam, and tadpole shrimps, freshwater and anadromous fishes, freshwater mussels, and freshwater snails; and non-obligate species, which include plants, amphibians, or reptiles such as turtles (some of which are more aquatic than others).

[q] The terrestrial indicator was computed as the total number of listed species minus the number of aquatic listed species and is therefore equal to the number of terrestrial listed species that are not also aquatic species plus the number of unassigned species. This computation was used in place of the number of terrestrial species in order to avoid double-counting of species assigned to both the aquatic and terrestrial categories.

Table 4. Indicators not used.

Potential indicator	Limitation
Stressor	
Housing in riparian areas	Thought to be largely captured by roads in riparian areas.
Industrial sites	Have not attempted to incorporate this vast database.
OHV use level	Have not found national data on this.
Cultivation in riparian areas	Thought to be largely captured by roads in riparian areas
Recent timber harvest	Have not found national data on this.
Feedlots	Have not found detailed national data[a].
Atmospheric deposition—Hg	Mercury deposition was only available for the East in the NADP data.
Recent severe burns	Some polygon coverages exist, but are incomplete and inconsistent. Most recent data are in point coverages.
Susceptibility to landslides	A data set is available (Godt 2001; Radbruch-Hall and others 1982), but it was judged to lack sufficient accuracy.
Stream and soil condition	
Average concentration of selected constituents	Insufficient number of gages measuring water quality within watersheds.
Length of stream on EPA impaired waters list	303(d) list of impaired waters is of inconsistent data quality.
Average temperature readings	Insufficient number of gages measuring water quality within watersheds
Recent mean annual flow as a percent of pre-settlement mean annual flow	Inconsistent, incomplete recent national data for 5th-level watersheds, missing data for pre-settlement flows.
Fish population by species	Lack of data
Soil quality	Lack of consistent and comprehensive data.
At-risk resource	
Trends in availability or quality of resources	Lack of consistent and comprehensive data.
Length of pristine streams	Lack of consistent and comprehensive data.
Recreational fishing visitor days	Lack of consistent and comprehensive data.

[a] The EPA maintains a Contained Animal Feeding Operations database, but it does not suit our purposes because not all CAFOs are listed and because the location data are of mailing addresses, which may be different from the locations of the actual operations.

the colinearity in two ways. First, in assessing a given problem, we do not include indicators that, across all watersheds, are strongly correlated with another included indicator, where we define strongly correlated as having a Pearson correlation coefficient (R) greater than 0.6. Second, the weights we assign to the individual indicators (described in the next section) were set partially in light of the correlations among the indicators. For example, if indicators for three human presence stressors are included and, in aggregate, are judged to account for 30 percent of the problem, the weights assigned to the individual indicators sum to reflect the 30 percent judgment.

Scaling and Weighting Procedures

When characterizing watershed condition, indicator variables must be combined to reach an overall assessment of the relative positions of the watersheds. Ideally a multivariate model would be available that, across all important ecosystems, accounted for all relationships between stressors and watershed condition as well as for interactions among the stressors. Because watersheds are so complex and onsite inventory is expensive, such a comprehensive model will be an unmet goal for many years to come. In the absence of such a model we would wish to at least quantify, for some of the most prevalent ecosystems, the relationship of each stressor to each resource at risk and to each major stream and soil condition variable. For example, the effect of road density on suspended sediment in streams would be described in a series of equations, one for each major soil type and physiographic class. Such equations would probably be nonlinear, reflecting critical points in road density beyond which suspended sediment increases more rapidly than at lower densities. Of course, such relations would depend not only on slope and geologic considerations, but also on the design, surface, and maintenance of the roads. As this example suggests, however, such quantification is also very complex.

Table 5. Background variables.

Variable	Approach
Size of watershed	Total area and total land area (excluding water bodies), in km^2.
Watershed elevation	Minimum, maximum, and mean elevation based on 30m DEM.
Precipitation	1961-1990 average annual precipitation from 2 km grid generated by the PRISM model.
Erosivity[a]	Rainfall-runoff erosivity factor R, in hundred ft-ton/ac/hour (Renard and others 1997). Erosivity is used not as an independent stressor, but rather to weight some other stressors that are exacerbated by erosivity.
Population in year 2000	Total area-weighted population from 2000 census tract data.
Land ownership	Percent of watershed in NFS land, other federal land, and private land based on 2003 USGS Federal Lands and Indian Reservations proclamation boundaries for non-NFS land and on detailed forest land ownership boundaries obtained in July, 2009, from the Forest Service's Automated Lands Project (ALP) for NFS land.
Land cover type	Percent of watershed in each of seven major land cover types (forest, rangeland, water, wetland, agriculture, developed, and barren) based on 300m 2001 NLCD (two of these are used as stressors).[b]
Riparian buffer	Percent of area in riparian buffer (see table 3 for details).
Slopes	Percent of area in slopes greater than 3% and greater than 45% (see table 3 for details).
Erosive soils	Percent of area in highly erosive soils (see table 3 for details).
Stream length	From medium resolution USGS 2004 NHD streams.
ESA species	The following categories of ESA federal status species from the NatureServe database (see table 3 for source): aquatic species other than listed, terrestrial species other than listed, listed species not assigned habitat values, other than listed species not assigned habitat values, listed aquatic obligate species, other than listed aquatic obligate species, and total number of federal status species (see Appendix B).
Impaired waters	Km of steam and area of water body within the watershed failing to meet criteria for designated uses, as listed under 303(d) in the EPA's TMDS tracking system, 2002.

[a] The R-factor (which is used in the revised USLE) is the long-term average of the annual sums across all significant storms during the year of the product of E and I, where E is the kinetic energy of a storm and I is rainfall intensity, measured as maximum 30 minute rainfall depth during the storm. The energy component is meant to represent sediment transport capacity, whereas the intensity component is meant to represent particle detachment capacity. We began with a digitized isoquant map (the isoquants are called isoerodents) developed in about 1998 by the NRCS and then used the ArcGIS "Topo to Raster" tool to interpolate the projected polyline shapefile to a 1km raster with continuous values for R-Factor, using iterative finite difference interpolation. This variable is used to weight selected stressors affecting sediment.

[b] The seven cover types are constructed from the following 2001 NLCD classes: forest (41, 42, 43), rangeland (52, 71), water (11, 12), wetland (90, 95), agriculture (81, 82), developed (21, 22, 23, 24), and barren (31).

Although such relationships are fairly well understood for some stressors in a few well-studied zones, they are not well understood across most stressors or across the full geographic scope of the current assessment.

Without detailed models showing the quantitative relationships between the independent variables and the measure of watershed condition (or, in our case, the measure of risk of impaired watershed condition), we are left relying on simplifying assumptions. Our principal simplifying assumption is that the relation between all indicators and watershed condition is linear—that the scales differ only by a constant slope and intercept. In other words, we assume that two different but equal-sized moves along an indicator scale (say in km of roads per km^2 of watershed) cause two corresponding equal-sized moves along the index of risk of impaired watershed condition.

Numerous procedures have been proposed for combining across stressors or other relevant variables when a quantitative multivariate model is unavailable (for analyses of several, see, for example, Ebert and Welsch 2004; Smith and others 2003; Zhou and others 2006). Such procedures would combine indicators in some way to achieve an overall measure of risk of impaired watershed condition. The procedures should deal with three issues that are encountered in creating an aggregate index: the units in which the indicators are measured may differ from one indicator to the next; the indicators may to some extent be correlated with each other; and the indicators may be of unequal importance in characterizing the dimension at issue, which in our case is risk of impaired watershed condition. We employ a rather simple procedure, roughly similar to that used in other recent assessments of watershed condition, which relies on scaling (also called normalization) to deal with the units of measurement issue, avoidance of indicators that are highly inter-correlated, and weighting to reflect the relative importance of the different indicators and to account for remaining inter-correlation.[18]

Very generally then, the procedure for forming the composite measure of risk involves: (1) measuring each watershed for each indicator; (2) selecting a set of watersheds (or portions of watersheds) to be compared and then scaling of values for each indicator in order to provide comparability of value range across indicators for watersheds within the set; (3) multiplying the scale values by weights, with the weights expressing principally the relative importance of the indicators to overall risk of impaired watershed condition (with higher weights indicating greater importance); and (4) additively combining the weighted values for the indicators for each watershed. This is sometimes called the "weighted sum" method.

With proper scaling of the indicator values, the scale values are dimensionless and the resulting aggregated index of risk is invariant to a positive linear transformation of the original indicator values.[19] For example, it will make no difference to the aggregate index whether developed land cover is measured in acres or in percent of total area, or roads in riparian areas are measured in meters per km^2 or miles per mi^2. Similarly, to take an interval scale variable, it would make no difference whether temperature were measured in degrees Celsius or degrees Fahrenheit.

We implement the procedure in an Excel workbook (RWI.xls, as described in the "Results and Analysis" section), where the individual steps of the procedure can be observed.[20] The procedure, described here in terms of whole watersheds, has the following six steps (note that this procedure was also used for the NFS portions of watersheds and for non-NFS portions of watersheds):

1. For each watershed, the value for each indicator (table 3) is computed. For all indicators, a higher value indicates a greater level of concern.

2. For each indicator, the watershed values are normalized. That is, they are transformed linearly to a scale ranging from 0 to 1 using $x_{i,n} = (v_{i,n} - v_i^{min}) / (v_i^{max} - v_i^{min})$ where $x_{i,n}$ is the scale value for indicator i in watershed n, $v_{i,n}$ is the value of indicator i in watershed n in whatever units were used for the indicator, and v_i^{min} and v_i^{max} are the minimum and maximum values for the indicator, respectively.[21,22] The values of v_i^{min} and v_i^{max} represent whatever set of watersheds is chosen to provide the context for comparison. When the basis for comparison is the set of watersheds being assessed, the resulting scale values range from 0 to 1. For ease of notation, this procedure for linearly scaling an indicator is indicated by Ω; thus $x_{i,n} = \Omega (v_{i,n})$.

3. Separately for each set of indicators (stressors and at-risk resources) and each problem, the scale values for the indicators are each multiplied by weights and the products are summed for each watershed, producing two sums for each problem for each watershed, one for each set of indicators. The weights specify the relative importance of the indicators. As implemented in RWI.xls, the weights of each set must sum to 1.

4. For each watershed and problem, the stressor and at-risk resource values of step 3 are each multiplied by weights and the products are summed.[23]

---

[18] Although we limit the set of indicators to those that are not highly inter-correlated, we do not go the next step and attempt to select a parsimonious set of indicators. Such an effort, which could be achieved using Principal Component Analysis or similar approaches, should be pursued if this assessment were to be followed over time by other national-level efforts to assess the risk of impaired watershed condition.

[19] By "positive" linear transformation we mean a linear transformation with a slope coefficient > 0.

[20] RWI.xlsx (for Risk of Watershed Impairment) and related material are available at http://www.fs.fed.us/rm/value/ watershedcondition.

[21] This transformation does not work if all of the values for a given indicator are identical, for in this case the minimum equals the maximum, resulting in division by zero.

[22] The scale values provide an interval scale metric. With an interval scale metric, the zero point has no absolute meaning (i.e., it does not represent the absence of the thing being measured), but differences between numbers have meaning (e.g., a difference of 0.4 in scale value is twice as large as a difference of 0.2).

[23] An alternative to the weighted sum approach would be to multiply the scale value of stressors by the scale value of at-risk resources. This approach essentially weights the stressor value by the at-risk resource value and vice versa. Compared with the weighted sum method, this approach more effectively separates those watersheds with a confluence of high stress and high at-risk resources from watersheds without such a confluence. However, a disadvantage of this approach is that differential weights for stressors and at-risk resources cannot be used (the multiplication of the stressor and at-risk resource scale values essentially weights each component equally).

The weights specify the relative importance of the two sets of indicators. The weights must sum to 1.

5. The previous two steps were used separately for each identified problem (sediments, nutrients, and toxics). Step 5 combines results of step 3 across problems, separately for each of the two sets of indicators. That is, for stressors and at-risk resources separately, the values of step 3 for the three problems are each multiplied by weights and the products are summed. The weights express the relative importance of the problems in characterizing overall risk of watershed impairment. The weights must sum to 1. The result is an index for stressors and another index for at-risk resources. Each index combines across problems, providing an overall indication of the relative position of the watersheds.

6. Then, to provide an overall watershed summary, for each watershed the stressor and at-risk resource values of step 5 are each multiplied by weights and the products are summed. The weights, which sum to 1, specify the relative importance of the two sets of indicators, as in step 4. (An identical watershed summary value can be computed by applying the weighting procedure of step 5 to the problem-specific values produced in step 4.)

The procedure is presented more precisely in table 6, assuming a population of watersheds (n), a set of stressor variables (i), a set of at-risk resources (j), a set of watershed condition problems (k), weights (w), a procedure for linearly scaling an indicator (Ω), and that s indicates stressors and r indicates at-risk resources.

The results of steps 3 to 6 (sums of weighted values, y, see table 6) are summarized for presentation in terms of scale values (x), ranks (R), percentile ranks (Pr), and risk levels (G). The scale values (x) are computed from y as they were from v in step 2, linearly transforming the y scale to a scale ranging from 0 to 1.

Table 6. Procedure.

Step	Computation
1	$v^s_{i,n}$ = value of watershed n for stressor i
	$v^r_{j,n}$ = value of watershed n for at-risk resource j
2	$x^s_{i,n} = \Omega(v^s_{i,n})$ = scale value of watershed n based on stressor i
	$x^r_{j,n} = \Omega(v^r_{j,n})$ = scale value of watershed n based on at-risk resource j
3	$y^s_{k,n} = \sum_i (w^s_{k,i} \cdot x^s_{i,n})$ = sum of weighted scale values for stressors for problem k of watershed n
	$y^r_{k,n} = \sum_j (w^r_{k,j} \cdot x^r_{j,n})$ = sum of weighted scale values for at-risk resources for problem k of watershed n
4	$y_{k,n} = w^s_k \cdot y^s_{k,n} + w^r_k \cdot y^r_{k,n}$ = sum of weighted values for problem k of watershed n
5	$y^s_n = \sum_k (w_k \cdot y^s_{k,n})$ = sum across problems of weighted values for stressors of watershed n
	$y^r_n = \sum_k (w_k \cdot y^r_{k,n})$ = sum across problems of weighted values for at-risk resources of watershed n
6	$y_n = w^s \cdot y^s_n + w^r \cdot y^r_n = \sum_k (w_k \cdot x_{k,n})$ = sum of weighted values of watershed n

Summary of results of step 6 (similar summaries are possible of the results of steps 3-5)

$x_n = \Omega(y_n)$ = scale value of watershed n
R_n = rank (y_n) = rank of watershed n
$Pr_n = \Phi(R_n)$ = percentile rank of watershed n
$G_n = \Psi(x_n)$ = risk level of watershed n

Thus, for example, each y from step 4 is transformed as $x_{k,n} = \Omega(y_{k,n})$ and each y from step 6 is transformed as $x_n = \Omega(y_n)$. Ranks are computed directly from y; identical ranks could be computed from x. Percentile ranks (Pr) simply group watersheds into categories; here we use five categories each containing 20 percent of the watersheds. Given 3672 watersheds, the 734 watersheds with the lowest y values, indicating a relatively low level of risk, would receive a Pr of 1, and the 735 watersheds with the highest y values would receive a Pr of 5. To summarize by risk level, the scale values (x) are partitioned using a procedure we designate as Ψ. Thus, for example, $G_n = \Psi(x_n)$, where G indicates risk level. RWI.xls allows up to a 6-point risk scale, with the partitioning of the 0 to 1 range of scale values into the risk categories defined by the user. For presentation here we use all six categories with the first five categories representing equally sized intervals across the bottom half of the scale value range and the last category representing the top half of the scale value range, as follows:

Rating	Scale value
1	0 to .1
2	>0.1 to 0.2
3	>0.2 to 0.3
4	>0.3 to 0.4
5	>0.4 to 0.5
6	>0.5 to 1

Using six equally sized intervals would preserve the interval scale information contained in the scale values. We deviate from the equal-interval approach for the top (highest risk) interval because, as will be seen in the results section, the upper half of the scale value range is populated by very few watersheds, due to the highly skewed scale value distribution. Compressing the top half of the scale into one risk category allows for additional distinctions within the part of the scale where the great majority of watersheds are found.

An objective procedure for assigning the weights (w_i^s, w_j^s, w^s, w^r, and w_k) would require a precise definition of watershed condition and a quantitative model expressing the relative contribution of each dependent variable to the overall measure of watershed condition (or to risk of watershed impairment). Lacking a precise definition and a quantitative model, the assignment of weights must rely on professional judgment in light of the available evidence. For the purpose of illustration, and for application in lieu of something better, we use the weights listed in table 7.

The stressor weights within a group sum to the group weights listed in table 8. The weights in table 7 express our understanding of the relative contribution of each of the available indicators to risk of impaired watershed condition. The weights can be altered easily in RWI.xls. Users may wish to enter their own sets of weights.

Erosivity, the impact of rainfall on the soil, is a factor like slope, in that it accentuates the effect of a stressor. The higher the erosivity of an area, the greater is the amount of erosion that is likely to occur, all else equal. Unlike slope, which is treated here as a dichotomous variable in its role in the effect of roads or cultivation on sediment movement (see table 3), we treat erosivity as a continuous weighting variable but an optional one. The user has the option in RWI.xls to weight the road, cultivation, grazing, mining, and fire hazard stressors by erosivity using a simple multiplication of the erosivity value times the stressor value (v_i) before the scale value of the stressor is computed.

Ordering of Watersheds

The ordering (rating and ranking) of watersheds was performed by problem (sediment, nutrients, toxics) for three geographical scales and for four land ownership categories. The geographical scales are individual NFS unit (national forest or grassland), NFS region, and the entire study area (the 48 contiguous states). Thus, for example, watersheds are ordered for the sediment problem (1) by NFS unit (producing 116 sets of orderings), (2) by NFS region (producing eight sets of orderings), and (3) for the entire study area (producing one ordering). The ownership categories are entire watersheds, NFS land, non-NFS land, and non-wilderness NFS land. Orderings for NFS land are critical because the agency's management actions are largely limited to NFS land. And within NFS land, orderings for non-wilderness land are most relevant both because non-wilderness land faces greater stresses than wilderness and because managers have more options on such land. The condition of non-NFS land is also relevant, because the agency may take action on NFS land to compensate for a problem on non-NFS land downstream, or may wish to work with partners to resolve problems off of NFS land. In addition, overall watershed orderings are useful for determining to what extent the combination of NFS and other land presents watershed-level problems. Crossing these two ordering breakdowns, based on geographic scale and

Table 7. Weights.

Indicator variable	Problem		
	Sediment	Nutrients	Toxics
A. Indicator variables			
Stressor			
Population density	0.10		0.05
Population growth	0.05		
Developed land cover		0.15	0.10
Housing density		0.10	0.05
Road density	0.10		0.05
Road-stream crossings	0.15		
Roads in riparian areas	0.05		
Roads on steep slopes	0.07		
Cultivation on gentle slopes	0.05		
Cultivation on steep slopes	0.15		
Cultivation – all slopes		0.45	0.30
Cultivation on highly erosive soils	0.08		
Livestock grazing	0.10	0.05	
Confined animal feeding		0.10	0.05
Other (mines, quarries, etc.) land cover	0.05		
Mines			0.30
Area of potential severe wildfire	0.05		
Atmospheric deposition		0.15	0.10
Dams			
At-risk resource			
Water bodies	0.40	0.40	0.30
Municipal water intakes	0.30	0.30	0.25
Wild & scenic rivers	0.10	0.10	0.10
T&E aquatic species	0.20	0.20	0.30
T&E terrestrial species			0.05
B. Indicator categories			
Stressors	0.7	0.7	0.7
At-risk resources	0.3	0.3	0.3
C. Problems	0.6	0.3	0.1

Table 8. Aggregate weights of stressor groups.

Stressor group	Problem		
	Sediment	Nutrients	Toxics
Development	0.20	0.30	0.20
Roads	0.37	0.00	0.05
Farm and ranch	0.30	0.55	0.35
Mining	0.05	0.00	0.30
Other	0.08	0.15	0.10
Sum	1.00	1.00	1.00

USDA Forest Service RMRS-GTR-251. 2010.

land ownership, results in 3 x 4 = 12 sets of orderings per problem, or 48 sets in all (table 9). In addition, the orderings for all three problems together were performed separately for stressors and at-risk resources, producing another 24 sets of orderings (see RWI.xls).

Watershed boundaries rarely coincide with NFS unit boundaries. Some watersheds are entirely contained within NFS units, but most watersheds also contain non-NFS land. Some watersheds contain land from two or three NFS units or even two or three NFS regions, but most watersheds are associated with only one NFS unit.[24] Further, NFS units may be made up of numerous non-contiguous parcels. The existence of multiple NFS units or regions within a single watershed complicates the process of ordering watersheds within a given NFS unit or region. To keep things simple, when more than one NFS unit was found within a watershed, the watershed was assigned to the unit with the largest amount of land in the watershed.[25]

Grouping a set of watersheds and comparing them for risk of watershed impairment begs the question, *should the watersheds in the set be compared?* One might argue that it is not helpful or even "fair" to compare watersheds that cannot be brought up to the same level of watershed condition. For example, should watersheds without attractive mineral deposits be compared with watersheds where mining is common and very profitable, or should watersheds with little erosion potential be compared with watersheds containing highly erodible soils? It may even be the case that the maximum potential level of risk in one watershed is below the minimum potential level of another watershed; is it not misleading to compare such watersheds? Our response is that these concerns are really about how the orderings might be used, and not about the orderings themselves. The orderings we present are orderings of what is, not of what might be. The orderings are useful in understanding the range of conditions that exist; they provide a context for beginning to consider watershed improvement decisions. However, the orderings are insufficient for deciding a future course of action. The decision of what to do about risk of watershed impairment must take into account not only what is, but also what can be and how much it would cost to get there. It may even be, depending on the relative costs of making improvements, that a given expenditure to improve watershed condition would be more effective on a low-risk watershed than on a high-risk watershed. Consideration of the benefits and costs of efforts to improve watershed condition is complex and best performed at regional and local scales.

Data Processing

The projection for all data layers is "USA Contiguous Albers Equal Area Conic" (ESRI ArcGIS version 9.3).

We used overlay analyses in ArcGIS to combine indicator data layers with the watershed polygons. Data were then summarized and totaled for each watershed and relevant subset (for example, NFS land) of the watershed.

Because of constraints imposed by computer hardware and software, the large datasets we had for some indicators could not be analyzed in whole. To circumvent this problem, we used a "While Loop" in a

Table 9. Sets of watershed orderings.

48 sets of watershed orderings are produced by crossing the following 11 breakdowns for the weighted combination of stressors and at-risk resources:

Problems
Sediment
Nutrients
Toxics
All three together

Geographic scales
Individual national forest or grassland
NFS region
Entire study area (coterminous U.S.)

Land ownership categories
Non-wilderness NFS land within the watershed
NFS land within the watershed
Non-NFS land within the watershed
All land within the watershed

---

[24] Based on our analysis of the 3672 watersheds at issue, 131 watersheds are made up entirely of NFS land and the other 3541 watersheds also have non-NFS land. Of the 3672 watersheds, 318 have land of more than one NFS unit (303 watersheds have land of two units and 15 watersheds have land of three units). Note, however, that these counts rely on our decision to exclude NFS units within a given watershed if those units accounted for very little of the basin area or appeared to result from an error in boundary delineation.

[25] An unavoidable result of this rule is that the surface area of NFS land in a given watershed, which gets assigned to a particular NFS unit, may exceed the actual surface area of that NFS unit within that watershed (because it includes surface area from other NFS units).

Python script to divide the datasets into smaller parts, perform analyses on each part, and then recombine the parts.

Results and Analysis_____

Results are presented in this report, in accompanying online tables and maps, and in the online Excel file called RWI.xls (see footnote 20 for the website address). Ratings and ranks for each combination of problem (sediment, nutrients, toxics) and geographic scale (NFS unit, NFS region, or entire 48 states) are available in the ordering sheets of the file RWI.xls. Unless stated otherwise, the results presented here are based on the weights listed in table 7 and do not use erosivity to further weight selected stressors.

A great many graphs or figures could be produced summarizing the data and related watershed orderings available in RWI.xls. In the accompanying online material, in addition to RWI.xls, we present the following information: a description of RWI.xls, tables of risk scale values and ranks by NFS unit, tables of numbers of threatened and endangered species by NFS unit, national maps showing levels of the indicators, national maps showing risk levels for whole watersheds, national and regional maps showing risk levels for non-wilderness NFS parts of watersheds, and region-level graphs of NFS unit scale values.

In considering the results that follow, it is important to realize that, although all regions contain some watersheds with very little NFS land and others that are completely made up of NFS land, the NFS regions differ in land ownership distributions, and fall roughly into three groups. The watersheds of the eastern regions tend to contain the least amount of NFS land; the median percent NFS is 18 percent in Region 8 and 21 percent in Region 9. The watersheds of Regions 2 and 3 contain slightly more NFS land; the median percent NFS is 25 percent in Region 3 and 30 percent in Region 2. The watersheds of the remaining regions tend to contain considerably more NFS land; median percentages NFS are 42 percent, 40 percent, 43 percent, and 46 percent in Regions 1, 4, 5, and 6, respectively. These percentages of NFS land reflect the history of land settlement prior to the parcels being set aside, which in turn reflects not only the human migration patterns and policies that influenced settlement, but also the climate and the topography, soils, and vegetative cover of the land, among other things.

Background information on watershed sizes, elevations, and ownership by region is given in Appendix A.

Relations Among Components of the Conceptual Model

Our approach to assessing risk of impaired watershed condition recognizes different watershed management problems, two broad sets of indicators (stressors and at-risk resources), and a set of individual indicators. Here we report on relations among these components of the approach.

Relations among problems

As described in the Methods section, the scale value range is partitioned into six intervals representing levels of risk. Combining across all stressors and at-risk resources, the whole watershed scale values ($y_{k,n}$, table 6) across the full set of 3672 watersheds form unimodal distributions for each of the three problems, as indicated by the assignment of watersheds to risk levels shown in table 10. Interestingly, the distributions for all three problems are highly skewed, with the mode at either the lowest risk level (nutrients and toxics) or the second risk level (sediment). Across all three problems, at least 60 percent of the watersheds fall within the lowest two risk levels (1 or 2) and fewer than 9 percent fall within the highest two risk levels (5 or 6). Clearly, a few watersheds stand out as facing relatively high risk in comparison to the bulk of the watersheds.

Across all 3672 whole watersheds, values across all stressors ($y_{k,n}^{s}$) for sediment are quite highly correlated with those of the other two problems (the correlations are 0.55 for stressors versus nutrients

Table 10. Distribution of whole watersheds by risk level and problem ($G_{k,n}$).

Risk level	Sediment	Nutrients	Toxics	All 3 problems
1	521	2206	1885	850
2	1667	481	695	1559
3	1015	444	470	667
4	344	272	306	342
5	82	140	174	175
6	43	129	142	79
All	3672	3672	3672	3672

and 0.58 for stressors versus toxics), and the values for nutrients versus toxics are very highly correlated ($R = 0.98$).[26] This indicates that the nutrient and toxic scales are not each making unique contributions to the overall characterization of watershed stressors. The correlations reflect in part the facts that some stressors contribute to more than one problem (for example, cultivation contributes to all three problems), and that different stressors tend to occur in tandem (for example, cultivation, housing, and mines all require roads). In addition, the correlations reflect the stressors and weights we used (listed in table 7), which in turn reflect our judgments about the risks that the stressors pose to watershed condition.

Turning now to at-risk resources, all three correlations among $y^r_{k,n}$ are very high (1.00, 0.96, and 0.96, respectively), which is not unexpected given that we used only five at-risk resources and that the weights we used are very similar across the three problems. If data on more at-risk resources were available, and if the additional at-risk resources were each uniquely affected by the different problems, the at-risk resource

category of indicators would contribute more to the distinctions among watersheds in the overall assessment of risk of impaired watershed condition.

Although the overall correlations across problems are rather high, this does not necessarily mean that the watersheds, or even the NFS units, rank the same for all three problems. To see this, consider as an example the NFS units of Region 2 for the three problems using the weights of table 7, and focusing on whole watersheds. Figure 6 presents the combined (stressors plus at-risk resources) scale values ($y_{k,n}$) for the 15 units of Region 2, where the scale values were computed relative to the range in scale values across the full set of 116 NFS units in the contiguous 48 states for each of the problems (the scale values for all of the regions are listed in the accompanying online material). Notice that the scale values are nearly all below 0.3, indicating that the watersheds associated with units of Region 2 fall in the lower part of the full range among units nationwide for each of the three problems. The nutrient scale values are particularly low, with all but four falling below a scale value of 0.1. As seen, the Region 2

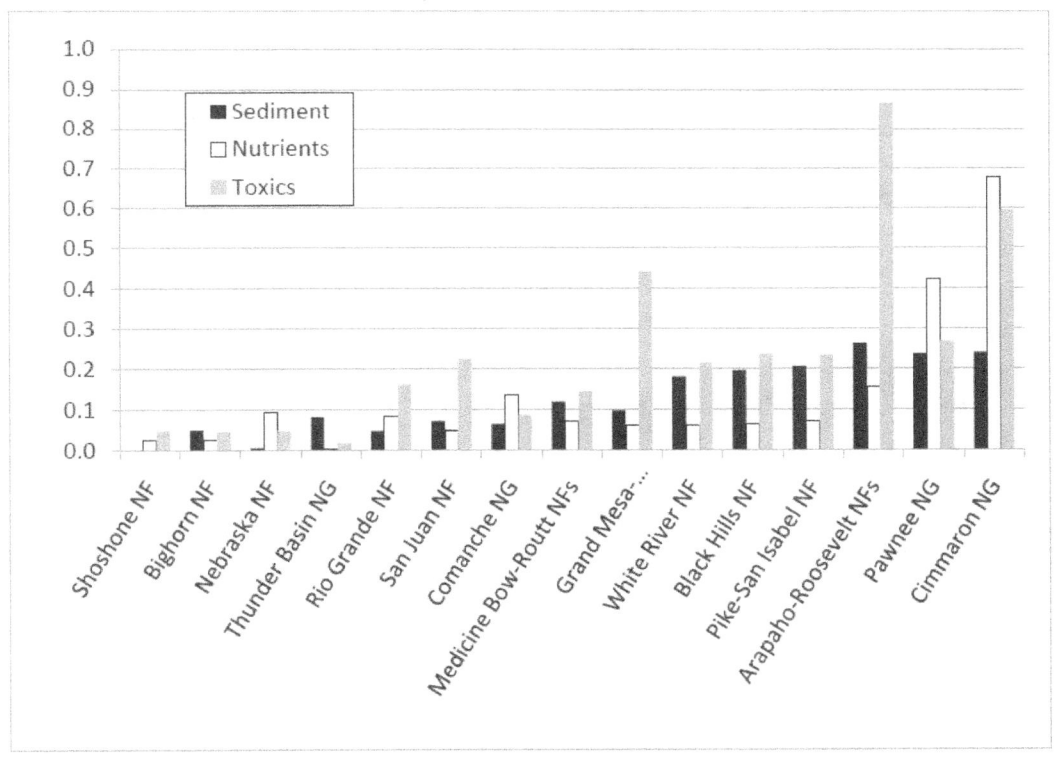

Figure 6. Scale values of whole watersheds containing NFS units of Region 2.

---

[26] Respectively, the corresponding correlations are 0.35, 0.44, and 0.93 for NFS parts of watersheds and 0.56, 0.60, and 0.97 for non-NFS parts of watersheds. The stronger relations for non-NFS lands result from the much greater importance of development and cultivation stressors, which both cause erosion and contribute nutrients, on non-NFS lands than on the NFS lands.

units rank quite differently depending on which problem is chosen. Note that the ranking based on the three problems together (indicated by the order of the units along the horizontal axis) is approximated by the order for the sediment problem, reflecting the relatively high weight given to the sediment problem (table 7).

Graphs similar to figure 6, but for non-wilderness NFS parts of watersheds, for the full set of regions are found in the accompanying online material, as are tables of the associated scale values. These graphs are also found in RWI.xls. The user may wish to enter a custom set of weights in RWI.xls and recompute the graphs.

Relations among indicators

Much could be said about the relations among the many indicators we investigated for the different sets of watersheds or parts of watersheds, but a thorough investigation of the relations among the indicators is beyond the scope of this report. Here we offer only a simple look at associations among indicators, to provide an initial understanding of how the stressors and at-risk resources relate to each other. For this purpose, we present correlation coefficients for two sets of watersheds or parts of watersheds, one for the full set of whole watersheds (table 11) and the other for NFS parts of the full set of watersheds (table 12). Both sets show simple correlations between pairs of indicators (both stressors, $y_{i,n}^s$, and at-risk resources, $y_{i,n}^r$). By and large, the correlations are rather low, indicating that in most cases the indicators are not simply duplicating each other, at least not across the full set of watersheds. However, some relations show expectedly higher correlations, especially for whole watersheds. These higher correlations generally reflect the fact that stressors often occur together (in proximity)—the result of the multifarious impacts that humans tend to impose on the land.

For whole watersheds, for stressors, the following correlations are of particular interest (table 11):

- Population density correlates highly with developed land cover (0.82), housing density (0.88), and road density (0.64), and quite highly with road-stream crossings (0.41).

- Road density is, as would be expected, quite strongly correlated with other road-related measures, such as road-stream crossings (0.78) and length of roads in riparian areas (0.62).

- Density of road-stream crossings, of course, is highly correlated with density of roads in riparian areas (0.81), but is also fairly strongly correlated with housing density (0.42).

- Livestock grazing and confined animal feeding are both quite highly correlated with measures of agricultural activity.

- Erosivity is highly correlated with atmospheric deposition (0.72). However, this correlation largely reflects broad regional differences, with high levels atmospheric deposition occurring where erosivity is also highest, and vice versa.[27]

- Fire condition class 3, mines, and "other" land cover are not highly correlated with any other stressors.

Among resources at risk, for whole watersheds the correlations are all very low except for that between listed aquatic T&E species and listed terrestrial T&E species (0.51) (table 11).

And comparing stressors with at-risk resources for whole watersheds, the highest correlations are those for drinking water intakes with population density (0.60), developed land cover (0.62), housing density (0.62), road density (0.52), and road-stream crossings (0.37).

Comparison of tables 11 and 12 reveals an interesting general difference: the correlations for whole watersheds tend to be higher than those for NFS parts of watersheds. For example, there are 64 correlations of at least 0.2 in table 11, but only 24 such correlations in table 12. The differences in magnitude of the correlations are confined to stressors and reflect two basic differences between the land areas being compared. First, stressors are more common and more interrelated on private land (which makes up the bulk of the non-NFS land) than on NFS land, in part because private land lacks many of the constraints on human pursuits that characterize NFS land management. Some activities on private land that cause stress to watersheds often occur in proximity, as do cultivation and livestock

---

[27] In watersheds of Regions 1-6, watershed average erosivity generally falls below an R-factor of 100 (although it reaches above an R-factor of 200 in a few watersheds of Regions 5 and 6) and atmospheric deposition is below 10 kg/ha, whereas in the two eastern regions erosivity is often above 200 (it ranges from 120 to 650 in Region 8 and from 75 to 259 in Region 9) and atmospheric deposition ranges from 11 to 47 kg/ha.

Table 11. Correlations among indicators for 3672 whole watersheds.[a]

	Pop. density	Population growth	Cover developed	Housing density	Road density	Rxs crossings	Road riparian	Road steep	Ag gentle	Ag steep	Ag all	Ag erosive	Grazing	Animal feeding	Other cover	Mines	Fire class 3	Atmospheric dep	Erosivity	Dams	Water bodies	Drink intakes	Wild & scenic	T&E aquatic	T&E terrestrial
Pop. density	1.00																								
Pop. growth	0.01	1.00																							
Cover,devel.	0.82	-0.03	1.00																						
Housing den	0.88	0.06	0.80	1.00																					
Road den	0.64	-0.06	0.80	0.62	1.00																				
Rxs cross	0.41	-0.01	0.60	0.42	0.78	1.00																			
Roads ripar.	0.26	0.00	0.37	0.26	0.62	0.81	1.00																		
Roads steep	0.04	-0.03	0.06	0.04	0.20	0.15	0.37	1.00																	
Ag gentle	0.03	-0.15	0.21	0.00	0.20	0.16	-0.03	-0.20	1.00																
Ag steep	0.02	-0.08	0.18	0.00	0.17	0.26	0.26	-0.06	0.33	1.00															
Ag all	0.03	-0.16	0.24	0.00	0.22	0.22	0.07	-0.19	0.94	0.62	1.00														
Ag erosive	0.00	-0.02	0.02	-0.01	0.02	0.05	0.07	-0.02	0.13	0.42	0.25	1.00													
Grazing	-0.01	-0.08	0.09	-0.04	0.09	0.10	0.01	-0.16	0.38	0.38	0.45	0.02	1.00												
Feeding	0.00	0.00	0.08	-0.01	0.07	0.05	-0.04	-0.10	0.32	0.20	0.34	0.00	0.56	1.00											
Other cover	0.02	-0.04	0.06	0.03	0.04	0.06	0.03	-0.02	-0.01	0.01	-0.01	-0.01	-0.03	-0.01	1.00										
Mines	-0.01	0.05	-0.03	0.00	-0.02	0.04	0.13	0.15	-0.09	-0.07	-0.09	-0.03	-0.09	-0.06	0.09	1.00									
Fire class 3	-0.06	-0.03	-0.10	-0.03	0.02	-0.02	0.09	0.20	-0.17	-0.08	-0.17	-0.05	-0.18	-0.08	-0.01	0.06	1.00								
Atmos. dep	0.03	-0.18	0.29	0.05	0.26	0.23	0.10	-0.14	0.28	0.39	0.37	-0.02	0.22	0.18	0.07	-0.10	-0.02	1.00							
Erosivity[b]	0.03	-0.13	0.26	0.05	0.25	0.07	-0.11	-0.07	0.26	0.15	0.27	-0.04	0.18	0.18	0.03	-0.08	-0.09	0.72	1.00						
Dams	0.03	0.00	0.32	0.18	0.27	0.21	0.09	-0.10	0.20	0.14	0.22	-0.01	0.11	0.07	0.09	0.02	-0.08	0.33	0.28	1.00					
Water	-0.01	-0.06	0.04	0.03	0.05	-0.01	-0.14	-0.12	0.01	-0.06	-0.03	-0.03	-0.07	-0.02	0.07	-0.06	0.16	0.22	0.23	0.01	1.00				
Drink intakes	0.60	0.02	0.62	0.62	0.52	0.37	0.25	0.08	-0.01	0.01	-0.01	-0.01	0.03	-0.02	0.01	0.00	-0.01	0.05	0.03	0.15	0.08	1.00			
Wild & scen	-0.02	-0.06	-0.01	-0.01	-0.03	-0.09	-0.05	0.16	-0.08	-0.04	-0.08	-0.02	-0.04	-0.04	-0.02	0.01	0.15	-0.01	0.01	-0.05	-0.02	-0.01	1.00		
T&E aquatic	0.08	0.04	0.15	0.11	0.09	0.07	0.05	0.09	-0.02	0.03	0.00	-0.01	-0.06	-0.03	0.00	0.05	-0.06	0.10	0.13	0.03	-0.02	0.09	0.07	1.00	
T&E terrest.	0.13	0.06	0.23	0.18	0.14	0.10	0.06	0.13	-0.08	-0.02	-0.07	-0.04	-0.08	-0.06	0.03	0.04	-0.11	0.11	0.15	-0.01	0.00	0.22	0.03	0.51	1.00

[a] Correlations of at least 0.034 and 0.045 are significant at the 0.05 and 0.01 probability levels, respectively.

[b] Erosivity is included here because it may be used in RWI.xls to weight selected stressors.

Table 12. Correlations among indicators for NFS parts of the 3672 watersheds.[a]

	Population density	Population growth	Cover developed	Housing density	Road density	Rxs crossings	Road riparian	Road steep	Ag gentle	Ag steep	Ag all	Ag erosive	Grazing	Other cover	Mines	Fire class 3	Atmospheric dep	Erosivity	Dams	Water bodies	Drink intakes	Wild & scenic
Pop. density	1.00																					
Pop. growth	0.04	1.00																				
Cover, devel.	0.35	-0.12	1.00																			
Housing den	0.13	0.03	0.15	1.00																		
Road density	0.04	-0.11	0.43	0.05	1.00																	
Rxs crossing	0.00	-0.01	0.17	0.03	0.52	1.00																
Roads ripar.	-0.02	0.00	0.06	0.00	0.50	0.56	1.00															
Roads steep	0.03	-0.01	0.18	0.00	0.34	0.13	0.24	1.00														
Ag gen le	0.09	-0.07	0.24	0.00	0.14	0.07	0.09	-0.09	1.00													
Ag steep	0.18	-0.07	0.17	-0.01	0.00	-0.03	-0.03	-0.06	0.19	1.00												
Ag all	0.13	-0.08	0.27	0.00	0.12	0.06	0.07	-0.09	0.95	0.48	1.00											
Ag erosive	0.02	-0.04	0.05	0.00	0.00	0.01	0.03	-0.02	0.02	0.17	0.07	1.00										
Grazing	0.06	-0.07	0.12	-0.01	0.03	0.00	-0.05	-0.12	0.11	0.21	0.17	0.01	1.00									
Other cover	0.07	-0.04	0.06	0.00	0.05	0.04	0.01	-0.02	0.01	0.02	0.01	0.01	-0.01	1.00								
Mines	-0.02	0.03	-0.04	0.00	-0.02	0.03	0.05	0.12	-0.04	-0.03	-0.05	-0.02	-0.07	-0.01	1.00							
Fire class 3	-0.07	0.00	-0.05	0.01	0.17	0.10	0.14	0.09	-0.07	0.04	-0.05	-0.03	-0.13	0.01	0.04	1.00						
Atmos. dep	0.36	-0.17	0.49	0.07	0.10	-0.03	-0.07	-0.15	0.18	0.37	0.27	0.09	0.18	0.06	-0.12	-0.05	1.00					
Erosivity[b]	0.29	-0.13	0.53	0.08	0.18	-0.03	-0.15	-0.06	0.19	0.22	0.23	0.01	0.16	0.06	-0.07	-0.12	0.70	1.00				
Dams	0.06	0.01	0.08	0.02	0.06	0.11	0.01	-0.06	0.05	0.06	0.07	0.00	0.06	0.00	-0.01	-0.05	0.07	0.04	1.00			
Water	0.03	-0.06	0.11	0.04	0.06	0.02	-0.08	-0.11	0.02	-0.03	0.01	-0.01	-0.07	0.00	-0.07	0.08	0.22	0.21	0.03	1.00		
Drink intakes	0.14	0.00	0.24	0.13	0.06	0.09	0.04	0.08	0.00	-0.03	-0.01	-0.01	0.02	0.00	0.03	0.01	-0.01	0.00	0.08	0.03	1.00	
Wild & scenic	0.08	-0.05	0.05	0.01	0.00	-0.05	-0.04	0.07	-0.03	0.00	-0.02	-0.01	0.00	-0.01	-0.01	0.07	0.05	0.03	-0.01	0.00	-0.01	1.00

[a] Correlations of at least 0.034 and 0.045 are significant at the 0.05 and 0.01 probability levels, respectively.

[b] Erosivity is included here because it may be used in RWI.xls to weight selected stressors.

feeding, tending to raise the inter-indicator correlations on non-NFS land. Second, stressors are least common on designated wilderness lands, which make up 17 percent of the NFS lands, tending to lower the correlations for NFS land.

It should be remembered that these correlations are for the entire set of 3672 watersheds and that correlations across watersheds of individual regions or NFS units may be quite different.

Relations between stressors and at-risk resources

We move now to a comparison of the two components of the conceptual model, stressors to at-risk resources. Are at-risk resources most numerous where stressors are most threatening, or are these two components of our conceptual model unrelated or possibly even negatively related? We explore these questions by examining the correlations of the summary values of stressors ($y_{k,n}^s$) with the summary values of at-risk resources ($y_{k,n}^r$) for the three problems (k). For whole watersheds, these correlations are 0.11, 0.10, and 0.12 for the sediment, nutrients, and toxics problems, respectively. For NFS parts of watersheds, the correlations are 0.02, 0.18, and 0.18, respectively. These low correlations indicate that the relation of stressors to at-risk resources is generally positive but weak, and thus that including both stressors and at-risk resources in the analysis is important, all else equal.

However, this finding does not apply to all regions, as there are significant regional differences. As shown in table 13, the correlations of stressors to at-risk resources tend to be positive in the western regions but are consistently negative in the eastern regions. Further examination reveals that the negative correlations result largely from the location of water bodies in the eastern regions. Watersheds with large numbers of water bodies in the eastern regions tend to be located away from development pressures, especially pressures from housing, roads, cultivation, dams, and atmospheric deposition. For example, consider the relation of water bodies to housing. In the eastern regions high water body density tends to occur at low housing densities, with little evidence of such a relation in the western regions. In Region 9, the most obvious case of this phenomenon is that of the lake country of northern Michigan, Wisconsin, and Minnesota, where nearly 40 percent of the Region's watersheds are found. In Region 8, this combination of high lake density and relatively low housing density is found in

Table 13. Correlation of scale value of stressors to scale value of at-risk resources, whole watersheds.

	Problem			
Region	Sediment	Nutrients	Toxics	All three
1	0.02	-0.08	-0.11	-0.05
2	0.22	-0.07	0.03	0.09
3	0.02	-0.02	0.01	0.00
4	0.08	0.17	0.11	0.13
5	0.45	0.50	0.55	0.52
6	-0.13	0.08	0.11	-0.05
8	-0.12	-0.22	-0.16	-0.18
9	-0.39	-0.53	-0.52	-0.52
All	0.11	0.10	0.12	0.12

areas of northern Florida and along the coasts of North and South Carolina.

In the western regions the correlations of stressors to at-risk resources are positive but generally quite low, with the exception of Region 5, where the correlations among the three problems range from 0.45 to 0.55 (table 13). The higher correlations for Region 5 are attributed largely to the stronger relations between the development, road, and cultivation stressors and aquatic T&E species.

Comparison of NFS Regions: Indicators and Background Variables

The NFS regions differ markedly in terms of many of the variables we measured. As a very general comparison of the regions, we present two tables for whole watersheds: one of background variables and the other of indicators.

First, table 14 lists area-weighted average values for background variables, providing a rough comparison of the ownership, cover, topography, and other basic characteristics of the regions. Some general observations from the table are:

- **Land ownership**. Only about one-fourth of the land area of the watersheds in Regions 8 and 9 is part of the NFS, far less than for the other regions, which range from 34 percent (Region 2) to 46 percent (Region 6) in the NFS. Other (non-NFS) federal ownership is greatest in Regions 3 (22 percent) and 4 (34 percent), lowest in the eastern regions (3 percent) (see also figure 5). For more detail on land ownership, see Appendix A.

Table 14. Values of background variables for NFS regions, whole watersheds.

Variable	NFS Region								All watersheds
	1	2	3	4	5	6	8	9	
Surface area (km²)	238,230	260,034	234,535	315,495	181,206	216,591	239,365	188,906	1,874,362
Precipitation (mm/yr)[a]	683	512	434	503	830	1215	1330	942	782
Population in year 2000 (1000s)	682	1,904	3,630	3,333	11,880	1,405	5,366	2,411	30,612
Erosivity (hundreds ft·tonf·in·(ac·h)⁻¹)[a]	17.55	21.40	32.87	8.27	34.40	38.66	308.65	126.82	70.70
% of area in NFS ownership	43.41	33.68	35.03	40.62	45.27	46.11	22.41	25.72	36.57
% of area in other federal ownership	8.40	14.90	21.58	33.71	13.43	12.16	2.59	2.95	14.84
% of area state & private ownership	48.19	51.42	43.39	25.66	41.30	41.73	75.00	71.33	48.59
% of area in forest cover	45.81	33.47	29.82	32.09	41.83	57.69	61.19	66.35	44.81
% of area in range cover	41.99	55.48	65.53	57.49	46.13	31.85	7.90	3.87	40.45
% of area in water cover	0.96	0.63	0.22	0.56	1.01	1.19	2.07	3.54	1.19
% of area in wetland cover	1.20	1.92	0.27	1.16	0.43	1.30	8.17	10.21	2.91
% of area in agricultural cover	8.17	4.97	1.43	5.16	2.59	4.06	14.40	11.28	6.47
% of area in developed cover	1.18	1.40	1.76	1.67	5.12	2.29	5.96	4.36	2.81
% of area in other (mines, etc.) cover	0.01	0.03	0.13	0.04	0.01	0.00	0.08	0.15	0.05
% of area in barren (rock, sand, clay) cover	0.67	2.11	0.84	1.84	2.88	1.62	0.25	0.24	1.31
% of area in riparian buffer	15.35	13.27	14.76	14.45	14.47	13.04	15.46	11.30	14.09
% of area with slopes > 3%	76.17	68.10	62.05	76.85	82.55	85.45	43.39	37.63	67.01
% of area with slopes > 45%	17.67	9.92	8.15	16.02	20.99	21.26	5.71	1.93	12.75
% of area with highly erosive soils	4.58	4.90	0.46	2.75	0.04	4.34	0.46	2.18	2.57
NHD stream length (1000 km)	188	177	176	232	133	143	190	110	1,349
303(d) Impaired streams (1000 km)	16	6	4	20	24	14	12	15	112
303(d) Impaired water bodies (km²)	881	77	76	213	421	128	1,055	2,762	5,611

[a] Area-weighted average.

- **Land cover**. The watersheds of the two eastern regions (8 and 9) have the highest levels of forest cover (over 60 percent of the area), wetland cover (about 9 percent), and agricultural cover (roughly 12 percent), and the least amount of rangeland cover (less than 8 percent). At the other extreme, Region 3 has the least amount of forest cover (30 percent) and the greatest amount of rangeland cover (66 percent). Regions 2 and 4 have slightly more forest than does Region 3 (about 33 percent), followed by Regions 1 and 5 at roughly 44 percent and then Region 6 at 58 percent, with rangeland cover correspondingly decreasing as forest cover increases. Wetlands cover less than 2 percent of the western region watersheds, whereas agricultural cover ranges from 1 percent (Region 3) to 8 percent (Region 1).

- **Riparian buffer**. The portion of the watersheds within the riparian buffer zone differs little across the regions, ranging only from 11 percent to 15 percent of the watershed area.

- **Topography**. The watersheds of the eastern regions have the gentlest slopes, with roughly 60 percent of the land having a slope no greater than a 3 percent. The watersheds in Regions 5 and 6 have generally the steepest slopes; in each region over 80 percent of the slopes exceed 3 percent and over 20 percent of the slopes exceed 45 percent. Regions 1 and 4 form the next group, where about 16 percent of the land is on slopes exceeding 45 percent, and Regions 2 and 3 form the final group, where about 9 percent of the land is on slopes exceeding 45 percent.

Table 15 lists area-weighted average values of the indicators by region for whole watersheds. Examination of table 15 reveals much about how the regions compare, offering a preview of the scale value results to follow. For stressors, Regions 5 and 8 have the highest levels of population density, developed land area, and housing density; Regions 5–9 have the highest levels of road density, road-stream crossings, and roads in riparian areas; Regions 5 and 6 have the highest densities of roads on steep slopes; Regions 8 and 9 have the highest percentages of land in cultivation; Region 3 has by far the highest densities of livestock grazing and confined animal feeding; Regions 5, 6, and 9 have the highest densities of land in fire condition class 3; Regions 8 and 9 have the highest levels of atmospheric deposition; and Region 8 has the highest

density of dams. Regions 1–4 stand out only for population change (Regions 2–4) and density of mines (with Regions 5 and 6 joining Regions 1–4 on this stressor). And for resources at risk, the greater densities are found in Regions 8 and 9 for water bodies, Regions 5 and 9 for drinking water intakes, Regions 5 and 6 for wild and scenic rivers, and Regions 6 and 8 for aquatic T&E species. Region 3 joins Regions 5–8 for high numbers of terrestrial T&E species. To summarize, in terms of regional averages, Regions 5–9 exhibit the greater levels of stress and at-risk resources.

As mentioned, tables 14 and 15 report on whole watersheds. Comparable values for NFS parts and non-NFS parts of watersheds are found in RWI.xls. Note that the regions do not differ one to the next as much in their NFS parts as in their non-NFS parts.

Focusing on whole watersheds, this section has examined variability across regions, which may be quite different from variability across NFS units within a region. To see this, consider the NFS units of one region, Region 2, for two indicators. Whereas mean density of roads in riparian areas varies from 1092 to 1632 among the eight regions (table 15), mean density of roads in riparian areas varies from 535 to 1604 m/km² among the 15 NFS units of Region 2. Similarly, whereas average density of mines varies from 8 to 28 mines per 1000 km² among the regions, it varies from 0 to 115 among the units of Region 2. Regional averages give an idea of how broad regions of the country differ, but mask the great variability within their boundaries.

How Levels of Indicators Differ by Land Ownership

Our data allow an important comparison between the risks faced on non-NFS portions of watersheds and the risks faced on non-wilderness NFS portions of watersheds (because many activities are prohibited in wilderness areas, they of course face less stress than other areas and are excluded from this comparison). This comparison provides a rough indication of the extent to which national forest designation provides a higher level of watershed protection than otherwise tends to be maintained. It is important to remember that non-NFS land is a mixture of state and private (77 percent) and federal non-NFS (23 percent) land, so that the comparison is not strictly a public-private one.

First we examine whether non-wilderness NFS parts of the watersheds are really different from the non-NFS parts. For the indicators and some additional

Table 15. Values of indicators for NFS regions, whole watersheds.

Variable	NFS Region								All watersheds
	1	2	3	4	5	6	8	9	
Population density (people / km^2)	2.89	7.35	15.51	10.64	66.38	6.56	23.14	14.06	16.65
Annual population change (%)[a]	1.83	2.65	2.75	3.05	1.12	1.89	1.48	0.95	1.60
Land cover – developed (% of area)	1.18	1.40	1.76	1.67	5.12	2.29	5.96	4.36	2.81
Housing density (units/km^2)	3.20	5.90	11.99	9.90	30.26	6.77	14.67	11.08	11.09
Road density (m/km^2)	772.01	852.11	882.06	724.01	1257.43	1159.50	1344.94	1173.38	991.20
Roads-stream crossings (#/stream km)	0.31	0.33	0.38	0.32	0.45	0.40	0.48	0.43	0.38
Roads in riparian areas (m/km^2)	1096.92	1139.32	1092.27	1114.09	1408.71	1631.64	1348.58	1234.67	1239.38
Roads on steep slopes (m/km^2)	55.45	13.62	8.96	22.51	81.84	106.86	26.70	8.72	38.61
Cultivation-gentle slopes (% of area)	6.55	3.92	1.34	3.86	2.09	2.36	10.19	8.21	4.75
Cultivation-steep slopes (% of area)	1.61	1.05	0.08	1.31	0.49	1.70	4.33	3.36	1.69
Cultivation (% of area)	8.17	4.97	1.43	5.16	2.59	4.06	14.40	11.28	6.40
Cultivation-erosive soils (% of area)	0.25	0.06	0.00	0.56	0.00	0.50	0.04	0.15	0.21
Livestock grazing (animal units/km^2)	5.55	7.23	4.03	4.54	6.14	4.04	11.99	6.79	6.23
Confined animal feeding (animal units/km^2)	0.05	0.83	0.63	0.17	0.02	0.05	1.74	0.51	0.51
Other land cover (mines, etc.) (% of area)	0.01	0.03	0.13	0.04	0.01	0.00	0.08	0.15	0.12
Mines (#/1000 km^2)	21.94	28.07	19.29	20.26	24.13	21.14	7.99	15.42	19.93
Fire condition class 3 (% of area)	18.76	11.21	17.35	9.38	23.88	22.60	8.33	36.56	17.21
Atmospheric deposition (NO$_3$ + SO$_4$ kg / ha)[a]	4.24	6.30	5.59	3.78	3.45	5.21	24.57	23.08	9.15
Dams (#/1000 km^2)	3.79	8.29	1.89	3.60	4.12	3.02	13.93	8.23	5.83
Water bodies (m of perimeter/km^2 of area)	51.39	38.84	16.16	42.63	65.79	44.56	211.36	610.64	121.16
Drinking water intakes (#/1000 km^2)	10.11	12.79	14.50	9.04	103.96	23.39	26.58	49.35	27.28
Wild and scenic rivers (m/km^2 of area)	3.65	0.63	1.37	1.05	10.95	9.19	4.19	5.65	4.12
T&E aquatic species (#/watershed)	1.08	0.90	2.56	0.91	1.71	2.63	2.82	0.79	1.65
T&E terrestrial species (#/watershed)	0.86	1.10	3.04	1.39	2.48	3.21	2.89	1.48	2.01

[a] Area-weighted average.

Table 16. Summary of non-wilderness NFS parts and non-NFS parts of watersheds.

Variable[a]	NFS		Non-NFS		t-test[c]	Correlation (R)
	Mean[b]	Median	Mean[b]	Median		
Area (km^2)	152.47	111.21	335.75	292.21	0.000	-0.31
Population density (p/km^2)	5.27	1.76	21.09	2.24	0.000	0.33
Annual population change (%)	1.64	1.35	1.65	1.35	0.047	0.94
Land cover – developed (% of area)	1.15	0.43	3.92	2.12	0.000	0.38
Housing density (units/km^2)	6.26	1.08	14.27	3.06	0.000	0.14
Road density (m/km^2)	746.37	666.84	1281.92	1148.73	0.000	0.23
Roads-stream crossings (#/stream km)	0.29	0.24	0.48	0.42	0.000	0.15
Roads in riparian areas (m/km^2)	1093.25	924.65	1555.57	1372.20	0.000	0.30
Roads on steep slopes (m/km^2)	62.54	16.16	46.05	7.92	0.000	0.58
Cultivation-gentle slopes (% of area)	0.40	0.00	5.95	1.25	0.000	0.47
Cultivation-steep slopes (% of area)	0.23	0.00	2.56	0.50	0.000	0.45
Cultivation (% of area)	0.63	0.00	8.43	2.65	0.000	0.45
Cultivation-erosive soils (% of area)	0.01	0.00	0.35	0.00	0.000	0.20
Livestock grazing (animal units/km^2)	4.99	2.94	6.76	4.29	0.000	0.85
Land cover – other (mines, etc.) (% of area)	0.01	0.00	0.08	0.00	0.000	0.12
Mines (#/100 km^2)	25.35	0.00	33.49	0.00	0.003	0.28
Fire condition class 3 (% of area)	22.59	11.70	15.89	4.68	0.000	0.71
Atmospheric deposition (NO$_3$ + SO$_4$ kg/ha)	9.09	5.10	9.25	5.25	0.000	0.96
Dams (#/100 km^2)	3.56	0.00	8.51	2.13	0.000	0.12
Water bodies (m of perimeter/km^2 of area)	115.41	0.00	146.96	21.02	0.000	0.71
Drinking water intakes (#/1000 km^2)	10.83	0.00	57.94	8.96	0.000	0.40
Wild and scenic rivers (m/km^2 of area)	4.15	0.00	6.48	0.00	0.000	0.38

[a] T&E species indicators are not included here because we have T&E data only for whole watersheds.
[b] Simple average across all 3541 watersheds with some non-NFS land.
[c] Probability for paired samples, two-tailed Student's t-tests comparing means.

variables, table 16 summarizes the comparison of non-wilderness NFS and non-NFS parts of the 3541 watersheds that contain land of both categories of ownership. For all of the variables listed in table 16, the mean value for the NFS parts of watersheds is significantly different from that of the non-NFS parts. Useful findings summarized in table 16 include the following:

- As one would expect, non-NFS parts of watersheds tend to have the greater densities of population, housing, roads, road-stream crossings, roads in riparian areas, livestock grazing, mines, dams, and drinking water intakes, as well as the greater land covers in cultivation and mining.[28,29]

- In contrast, NFS parts of watersheds have the greater density of roads on steep slopes and greater occurrence of forests in fire condition class 3.[30]

- As expected, the correlations for indicators of NFS parts versus non-NFS parts of watersheds are positive, suggesting that where the non-NFS portions are under higher levels of stress or contain higher numbers of resources at risk, so also are the NFS portions.

Looking beyond the measures of central tendency in table 16, with our data we can examine how the distributions for individual indicators differ between NFS and non-NFS parts of watersheds. As an

---

[28] The population density on NFS lands is an over-estimate resulting from our methods. Recall that population density was computed by averaging across census tracts. When census tracts span a boundary between NFS and non-NFS land, some of the population residing outside the national forest will unavoidably be counted as being in the national forest.

[29] The estimate of cultivation on NFS lands (0.25%) is perhaps slightly over-estimated because the land area coverage is a grid, and grid cell boundaries do not necessarily match NFS boundaries. However, some cultivation on NFS land would remain even without this problem. For example, some areas of the NFS were formerly cropped or mined and are still being rehabilitated, and some recent land acquisitions have yet to undergo rehabilitation.

[30] This finding reflects in part the differences in topography between NFS and non-NFS parts of the watersheds. Across all watersheds, 7% of the non-NFS land and 20% of non-wilderness NFS land is on slopes > 45%.

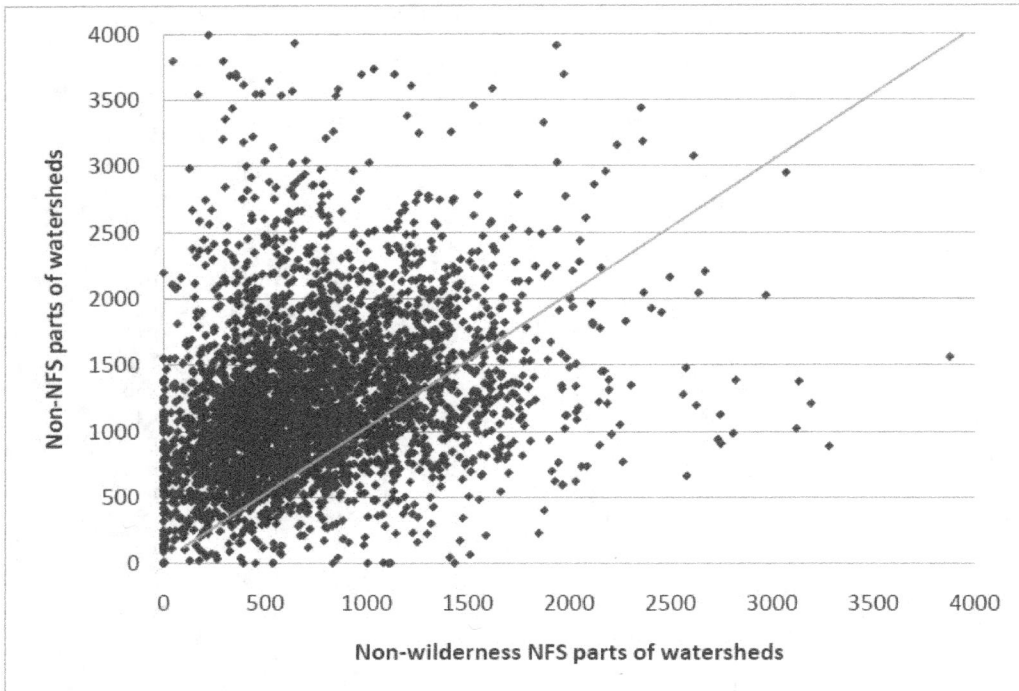

Figure 7. Comparing NFS and non-NFS parts of watersheds for road density (m/km²).

example we present a graph depicting how average road density compares on non-wilderness NFS and non-NFS lands across the 3541 watersheds with both categories of land (figure 7). A few extreme points are excluded, so that the range can be reduced sufficiently to more clearly show the distribution for the majority of watersheds. As expected, road density tends to be considerably greater on as opposed to off NFS land. Mean road density averages 746 and 1282 m/km² on non-wilderness NFS and non-NFS land, respectively (table 16). Mean road density is less on NFS land than on non-NFS land on 81 percent of the 3541 watersheds. It is perhaps surprising that road density is greater on than off of NFS land on 19 percent of the watersheds. Certainly the presence of other public land or large private holdings helps explain this finding, but it must also be noted that some NFS areas also have high road densities, particularly in Region 6.[31]

Moving from the national to the regional scale, table 17 contains a comparison of non-wilderness NFS and non-NFS lands for a selection of indicators, this time based on all available watersheds (i.e., the full set of 3672 watersheds for non-wilderness NFS land and

the 3541-watershed subset for non-NFS land). Considerable variation is found. Specific findings from table 17 include the following:

- Mean density of roads and road-stream crossings is greater off than on NFS lands in all regions. However, the regions differ in the extent to which these two categories of land differ. Mean road density on non-wilderness NFS lands is one-half or less than half of what it is on non-NFS lands in Regions 1, 2, 4, 5, and 8, but reaches to 80 percent of non-NFS density in Region 6. Region 6 also has the smallest difference between NFS and non-NFS lands in density of road-stream crossings.

- The average density of roads in riparian areas is greater on non-NFS lands than on non-wilderness NFS lands in all regions.

- Density of roads on steep (> 45 percent) slopes is greater on non-wilderness NFS lands than on non-NFS lands in all regions except Region 9. The highest densities for both categories of land ownership are in Region 6 (156 and 87 m per km² on non-wilderness NFS and non-NFS lands, respectively).

---

[31] For example, over half of the watersheds containing parts of six Region 6 NFS units (Fremont-Winema, Malheur, Ochoco, Olympic, Umatilla and Wallowa-Whitman NFs) have higher road densities on the national forests than off. It should be added, however, that in a few cases in these national forests as well as others the portions of the watersheds within the NFS are so small that the density estimate may not be representative of the condition of the national forest to which the specific NFS parts belong.

Table 17. Area weighted average values of selected indicators for NFS regions, non-wilderness NFS parts and non-NFS parts of watersheds.[a]

Indicator		NFS Region								All watersheds
		1	2	3	4	5	6	8	9	
Road density (m/km²)	NFS	622	563	670	471	922	1236	783	863	747
	Non-NFS	984	1057	1040	951	1698	1282	1514	1312	1204
Roads-stream crossings (#/stream km)	NFS	0.24	0.23	0.32	0.24	0.31	0.40	0.26	0.24	0.28
	Non-NFS	0.39	0.38	0.43	0.40	0.60	0.45	0.53	0.48	0.45
Roads in riparian areas (m/km²)	NFS	1030	979	1093	1080	1125	1666	869	862	1117
	Non-NFS	1263	1277	1165	1236	1819	1819	1481	1354	1392
Roads on steep slopes (m/km²)	NFS	106	22	16	41	121	156	36	9	68
	Non-NFS	32	11	5	14	69	87	24	9	27
Livestock grazing (animal units/km²)	NFS	3.03	4.78	2.19	3.51	5.17	3.15	8.46	4.19	4.05
	Non-NFS	7.67	8.80	5.03	5.52	6.22	4.96	13.02	7.78	7.60
Other land cover (mines, etc.) (% of area)	NFS	0.00	0.01	0.01	0.00	0.00	0.00	0.00	0.01	0.00
	Non-NFS	0.03	0.03	0.19	0.06	0.01	0.01	0.10	0.20	0.08
Mines (#/1000 km²)	NFS	29	27	23	28	32	24	6	8	24
	Non-NFS	20	31	18	16	21	17	9	18	19
Fire condition class 3 (% of area)	NFS	30	21	29	14	34	32	8	44	26
	Non-NFS	9	7	10	6	17	17	8	33	13
Atmospheric deposition ($NO_3 + SO_4$ kg/ha)	NFS	4.0	6.4	5.2	3.6	3.2	5.0	24.5	22.5	7.7
	Non-NFS	4.5	6.3	5.8	3.9	3.6	5.1	24.6	23.5	10.2
Dams (#/1000 km²)	NFS	1.2	8.0	1.1	2.5	2.9	1.9	3.8	3.4	3.0
	Non-NFS	5.7	9.1	2.4	4.5	5.5	4.0	16.9	10.0	7.7
Water bodies (m of perimeter/km² of area)	NFS	31	29	14	30	54	28	246	722	103
	Non-NFS	63	40	18	46	75	54	202	549	130
Drinking water intakes (#/1000 km²)	NFS	2.4	7.5	4.4	4.2	35.7	7.4	6.8	12.1	9.2
	Non-NFS	16.5	16.2	20.2	12.8	167.1	38.3	32.4	62.9	38.7
Wild and scenic rivers (m/km² of area)	NFS	4.1	1.3	1.3	0.8	13.4	10.8	7.5	11.7	5.7
	Non-NFS	1.4	0.3	1.1	0.2	8.0	6.8	3.0	3.9	2.6

[a] Based on all available watersheds (thus, the full set of 3672 watersheds for NFS land and the 3541-watershed subset for non-NFS land). Because area-weighted averages are reported here, the averages for non-NFS parts of watersheds will not tend to agree with the corresponding estimates in table 16, which are simple averages.

- Averaging over all watersheds, grazing density is nearly twice as high off of the NFS as it is in non-wilderness NFS parts of the watersheds. Average livestock grazing density is greater off, as opposed to on, NFS lands in all regions. Of course, these calculations depend in part on our assumptions in allocating county-wide data to the watersheds (see table 3).

- The density of mines is greater on non-wilderness NFS lands than off of the NFS in five regions, with the reverse being true in Regions 2, 8, and 9.

- The prevalence of drinking water intakes is much greater off than on NFS lands in all regions.

- Water bodies are more common in the eastern than the western regions. The average density of water bodies is greater on non-wilderness NFS than on non-NFS parts of the watersheds in the eastern regions, but the reverse is true in the western regions.

- Region 3 stands out as having the smallest difference between NFS and non-NFS lands for five indicators: density of roads in riparian areas, mines, dams, water bodies, and wild and scenic rivers.

Although we do not provide a detailed comparison of wilderness land versus non-wilderness land, we do not wish to leave the impression that designated wilderness is devoid of present or past activities that may affect current watershed condition. For example, of the 105 NFS units with wilderness acreage, our data show that 103 have roads, 75 have mines, 39 have dams, and 31 have drinking water intakes within one or more wilderness areas. Many of the roads may now be closed to all use, but some are used for specified purposes such as wildlife or livestock management or to access mines or other facilities. Most of the mines are abandoned, but some are still active. Details of the exceptions to the normal operating procedures for wilderness areas are written into the legislation authorizing the wilderness areas.[32]

Risk of Impaired Watershed Condition

As described in the Methods section, two ways to succinctly summarize watershed scale values are to (1) divide the scale value range into intervals and observe which watersheds fall within each interval (the G

scale), and to (2) divide the watersheds into essentially equal-sized subsets based on the scale values (the Pr scale). Both approaches yield useful information about the relative risk levels of the watersheds. The former approach highlights the interval scale nature of the scale values, wherein the watersheds may not be evenly spread along the range. Each interval represents a separate risk level that is directly comparable to the other risk levels. The latter approach emphasizes the ordinal position of the watersheds and provides what is perhaps the most easily interpreted summary of the findings. We apply both approaches here based on the summary scale values of the watersheds or parts of watersheds. Summary scale values are those that combine across the three problems (y_n, table 6). This is done across the coterminous United States for the following three sets of watersheds or parts of watersheds: whole watersheds, non-wilderness NFS parts of watersheds, and non-NFS parts of watersheds.

As explained earlier, for the former approach we have divided the 0 to 1 scale value range into the following six intervals: 0 to 0.1, >0.1 to 0.2, >0.2 to 0.3, >0.3 to 0.4, >0.4 to 0.5, and >0.5 to 1. Watersheds whose summary scale values fall into these intervals are assigned risk levels of 1, 2, 3, 4, 5, and 6, respectively. And for the percentile rank approach, we have used five quantiles (called quintiles) each representing 20 percent of the watersheds (or parts of watersheds) in the set. The 20 percent of the watersheds at lowest risk fall in quintile 1, the next 20 percent fall in quintile 2, etc. Assignment to quintile 5 indicates that the watershed is among the 20 percent of the watersheds at greatest risk of impaired condition.

Comparison of watersheds

Using the first approach just described, figure 8 shows the risk levels for the non-wilderness NFS parts of all watersheds, and table 18 summarizes the risk levels by region. In the table it is seen that the bulk of the watersheds fall in the lower two risk levels (thus, representing a scale value ≤ 0.2). For example, focusing on non-wilderness NFS parts of watersheds, only 29 percent the watersheds receive a risk level > 0.2 (table 18b). A few of the watersheds stand out as facing an unusual level of risk of impaired watershed condition, leaving most watersheds to fall in the bottom two

---

[32] An excellent searchable database of information about the special provisions affecting wilderness area management is available at www.wilderness.net, "tools for managers," "special provisions."

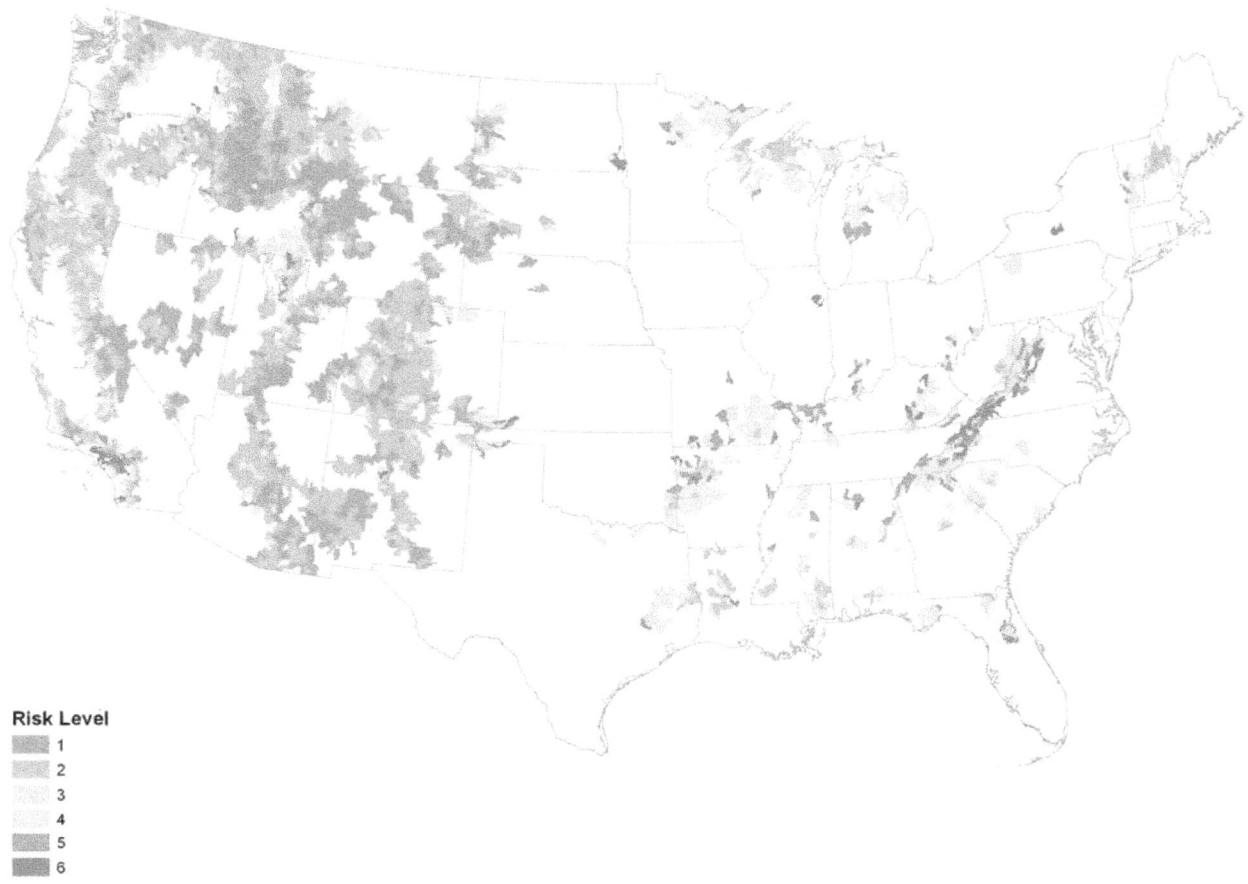

Risk Level
1
2
3
4
5
6

Figure 8. Comprehensive assessment of risk levels for non-wilderness NFS parts of watersheds (G_n), with scale values computed relative to the range across the full set of 3672 watersheds.

risk levels. For non-wilderness NFS land, these few watersheds are found largely in Regions 8 and 9.

It is important to remember that for this analysis the watersheds, or parts of watersheds (such as the non-wilderness NFS parts), in each set are scaled relative to others in the set, not relative to watersheds of another set, and thus that results for the different sets are not directly comparable across set.

Because the scale value distribution is so skewed, dividing the watersheds into only six groups—even after collapsing the top half of the scale value range into one risk category—does not allow for much distinction among the bulk of the watersheds, leading us to the quantile approach, presented in figure 9 and table 19. Examination of table 19 shows that the distributions of watersheds among the regions tend to fall into the following three groups: the eastern regions (8 and 9), with many watersheds in the higher quintiles, the intermountain regions (1 to 4), with relatively few

watersheds in the higher quintiles, and the West Coast regions (5 and 6), which fall in between these two extremes. These three groups contain 839, 1934, and 899 watersheds, respectively. Figure 10 summarizes the results for these three regional groups for non-wilderness NFS parts of watersheds. As seen in the figure, watersheds in the eastern regions account for nearly three-quarters (73 percent) of the watersheds in the fifth (highest risk) quintile (64 percent of the watersheds of the eastern regions fall in the fifth quintile). Watersheds falling in the fourth quintile are rather evenly spread among the three groups. Watersheds falling in the lowest three quintiles are mainly from the intermountain regions; these watersheds make up nearly all of the lowest two risk quintiles and most of the third quintile (note, however, that over half of the 3672 watersheds are in the intermountain regions). Sixty-three percent of the West Coast watersheds fall in the third and fourth quintiles.

Table 18. Number of watersheds by risk level by region, watershed sets scaled separately.[a]

Table 18a. Whole watersheds.

Region	Risk level						Total
	1	2	3	4	5	6	
1	156	244	66	21	3	4	494
2	142	250	44	18	5	1	460
3	125	204	17	6	3	1	356
4	299	229	52	27	12	5	624
5	79	220	90	20	12	12	433
6	47	294	100	12	11	2	466
8	0	70	182	127	72	38	489
9	2	48	116	111	57	16	350
Total	850	1559	667	342	175	79	3672

Table 18b. Non-wilderness NFS parts of watersheds.

Region	Risk level						Total
	1	2	3	4	5	6	
1	226	239	25	2	2	0	494
2	122	296	31	10	1	0	460
3	74	258	23	1	0	0	356
4	313	284	26	1	0	0	624
5	54	247	107	20	3	2	433
6	21	301	133	9	1	1	466
8	3	76	308	85	15	2	489
9	10	78	129	106	20	7	350
Total	823	1779	782	234	42	12	3672

Table 18c. Non-NFS parts of watersheds.

Region	Risk level						Total
	1	2	3	4	5		
1	73	237	72	31	17	8	438
2	89	226	92	29	9	7	452
3	137	161	29	17	5	3	352
4	222	219	80	21	16	30	588
5	69	176	109	34	13	23	424
6	62	210	115	38	13	13	451
8	1	41	129	139	95	82	487
9	2	27	99	109	66	46	349
Total	655	1297	725	418	234	212	3541

[a] The watersheds of each set were separated into six groups based on where their summary scale values fall along the scale value range. A risk value of 6 indicates the highest risk level.

How risk values differ by land ownership

In the previous section about summary scale values, the different sets of watersheds and parts of watersheds were scaled separately. In this section we combine all non-wilderness NFS parts and all non-NFS parts of watersheds in one data set and scale them together, allowing a direct comparison of these categories of land ownership across the coterminous United States.

Figure 11 shows the basic result of this rescaling, using the former (risk level) approach of the previous section, which places the watersheds into six groups each representing an interval along the scale value range. As seen in the figure, the distributions of the two sets of watershed parts are quite different.

The top four risk levels are largely populated by non-NFS parts of watersheds (indeed, 93 percent of the

Table 19. Number of watersheds by risk quintile by region, watershed sets scaled separately.[a]

Table 19a. Whole watersheds.

| Region | Risk quintile | | | | | Total |
	1	2	3	4	5	
1	138	119	116	84	37	494
2	114	136	123	57	30	460
3	102	125	89	30	10	356
4	266	161	84	58	55	624
5	73	80	108	117	55	433
6	39	92	166	125	44	466
8	0	15	27	166	281	489
9	2	6	22	97	223	350
Total	734	734	735	734	735	3672

Table 19b. Non-wilderness NFS parts of watersheds.

| Region | Risk quintile | | | | | Total |
	1	2	3	4	5	
1	206	122	103	49	14	494
2	108	159	125	48	20	460
3	66	113	116	49	12	356
4	274	209	89	45	7	624
5	50	57	113	141	72	433
6	19	59	134	180	74	466
8	2	1	21	150	315	489
9	9	14	34	72	221	350
Total	734	734	735	734	735	3672

Table 19c. Non-NFS parts of watersheds.

| Region | Risk quintile | | | | | Total |
	1	2	3	4	5	
1	83	119	124	69	43	438
2	100	132	108	76	36	452
3	146	109	54	25	18	352
4	234	140	87	64	63	588
5	74	88	110	97	55	424
6	67	95	147	97	45	451
8	1	17	38	163	268	487
9	3	8	40	117	181	349
Total	708	708	708	708	709	3541

[a] The watersheds of each set were separated into five approximately equal-sized groups based on summary scale values of risk. The 20% of the watersheds at lowest risk are assigned a risk level of 1, the next 20% are assigned a risk level of 2, etc. Thus, a risk level of 5 indicates that the watershed is among the 20% of the watersheds at greatest risk of impaired condition.

watershed parts with a risk level above 3 are on non-NFS land), and the two lowest risk levels are dominated by non-wilderness NFS parts. However, although NFS parts dominate at the lower risk levels, many non-NFS parts are also found at these low risk levels. For example, although 36 percent of the NFS parts (representing 1325 watersheds) fall in the lowest risk category, so too do 16 percent of the non-NFS parts (representing 560 watersheds). Thus, these 560 non-NFS parts of watersheds are found to be at lower risk than 64 percent of the non-wilderness NFS parts. Table 20 breaks the result down by region, showing, for example, that nearly all watershed parts, whether NFS or non-NFS, assigned a risk level above 1 are found in Regions 1–6.

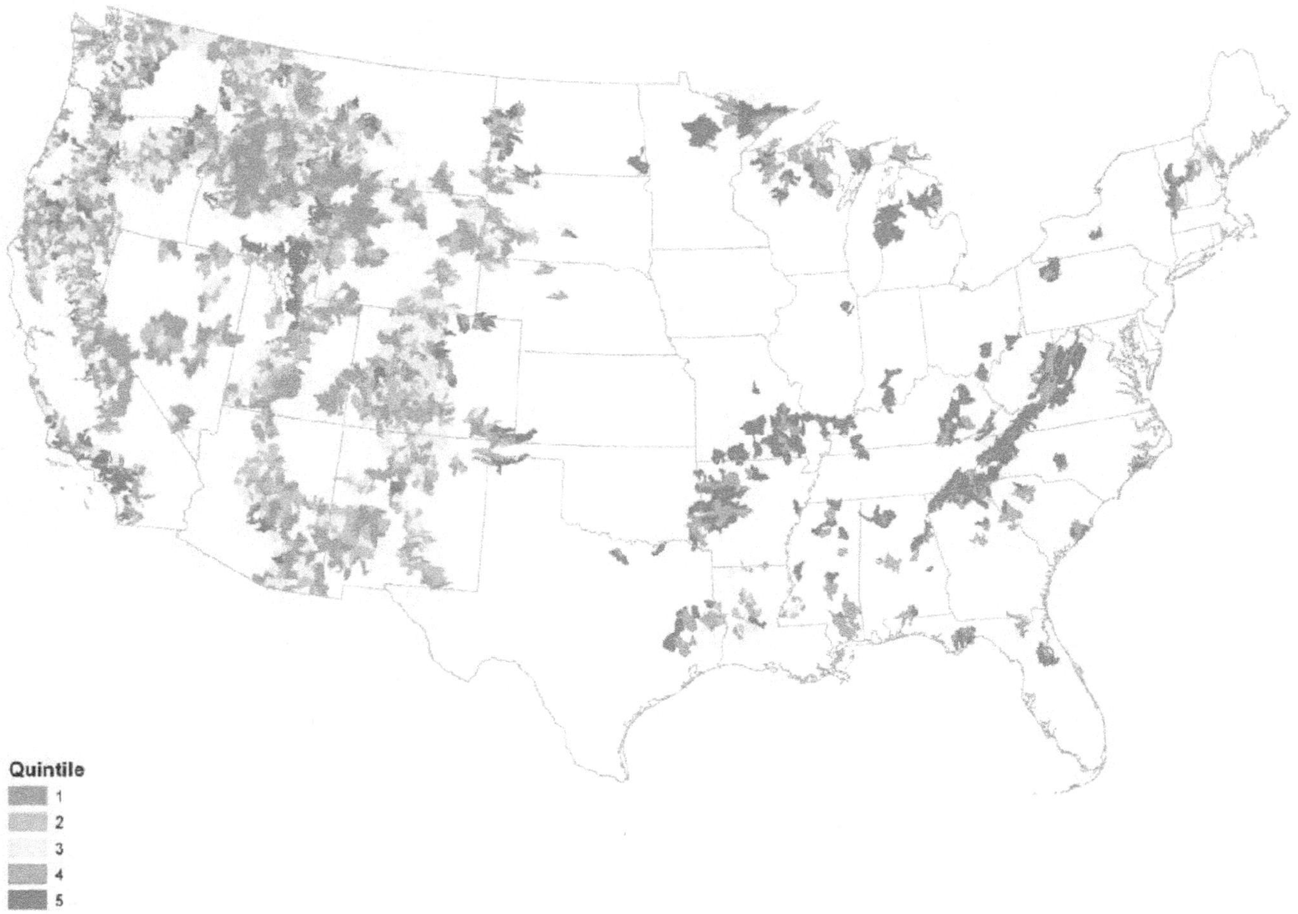

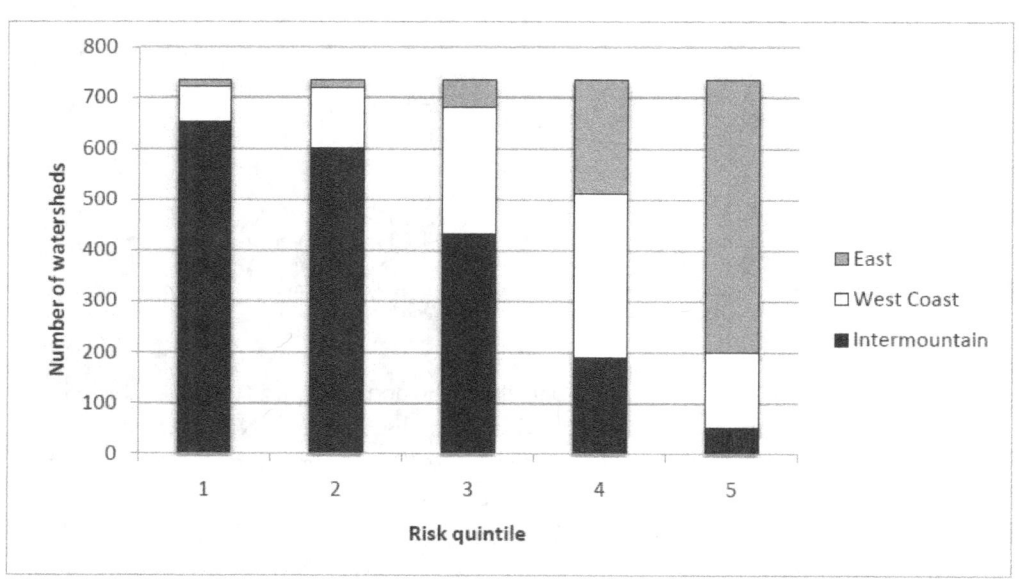

Figure 9. Risk quintiles for non-wilderness NFS parts of watersheds (G_n), with scale values computed relative to the range across the full set of 3672 watersheds.

Figure 10. Number of watersheds by risk quintile for three regional groups, non-wilderness NFS parts of watersheds.

USDA Forest Service RMRS-GTR-251. 2010.

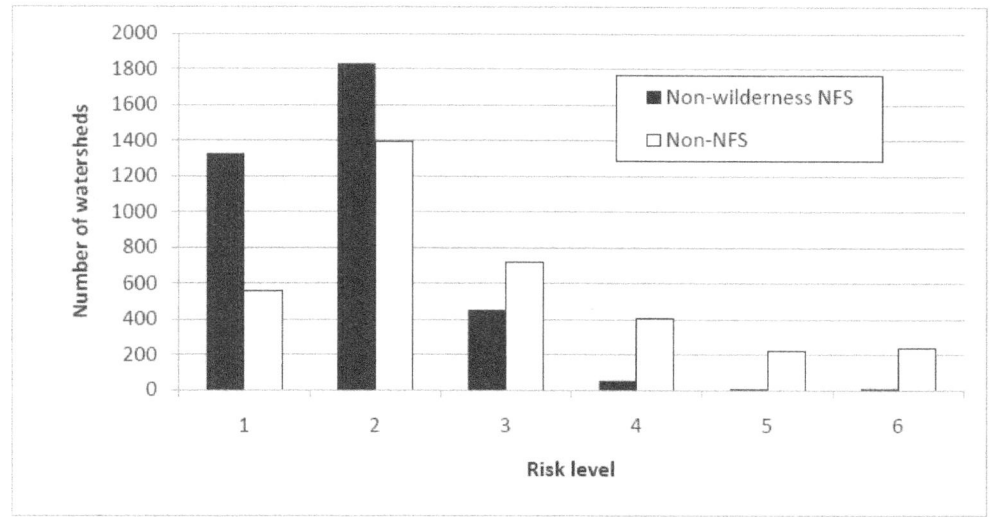

Figure 11. Number of watersheds by risk level.

Table 20. Number of watersheds by risk level by region, watershed sets scaled together.[a]

Table 20a. Non-wilderness NFS parts of watersheds.

	Risk level						
Region	1	2	3	4	5	6	Total
1	296	189	7	2	0	0	494
2	223	219	16	2	0	0	460
3	137	213	6	0	0	0	356
4	443	180	1	0	0	0	624
5	126	282	25	0	0	0	433
6	79	357	29	0	0	1	466
8	4	270	197	14	4	0	489
9	17	120	170	34	2	7	350
Total	1325	1830	451	52	6	8	3672

Table 20b. Non-NFS parts of watersheds.

	Risk level						
Region	1	2	3	4	5	6	Total
1	60	240	76	31	20	11	438
2	67	237	99	29	12	8	452
3	121	181	25	18	4	3	352
4	192	249	78	22	13	34	588
5	61	195	97	33	18	20	424
6	57	220	111	37	13	13	451
8	1	35	122	142	94	93	487
9	1	40	111	89	52	56	349
Total	560	1397	719	401	226	238	3541

[a] All watershed parts (i.e., both sets) were scaled together and then separated into six groups based on where the summary scale values fell along the scale value range. A risk value of 6 indicates the highest risk level.

Comparison of NFS units

Unlike the prior two sections, which report on the number of watersheds by region at different risk levels, here we report on average values across the watersheds within a NFS unit. Perhaps the most parsimonious way to compare NFS units is to observe summary scale values (that is, values combining across the three problems) with the units scaled to range from 0 to 1 relative to the range across the full set of 116 units (y_n, where n is a NFS unit). Figure 12 depicts these summary scale values, one dot per unit with the units arranged by region in order of increasing scale value from left to right. Figure 12a depicts scale values for whole watersheds, and figure 12b depicts scale values for non-wilderness NFS parts of watersheds. Note that in both figures the scale values range from 0, indicating the unit with the lowest risk of impaired watershed condition, to 1, indicating the unit with the highest risk. The scale values of each figure are internally consistent but not comparable across figures (for example, a scale value of 1 in figure 12a does not necessarily indicate the same level of risk as does a scale value of 1 in figure 12b).

As seen in figure 12a, only 15 units, found in Regions 5 through 9, have a scale value above 0.5. Regions 1, 3, and 4 exhibit a narrow range in scale value across their respective units, with no units having a scale value above 0.3. At the other extreme,

Figure 12. Summary scale values of NFS units by region.

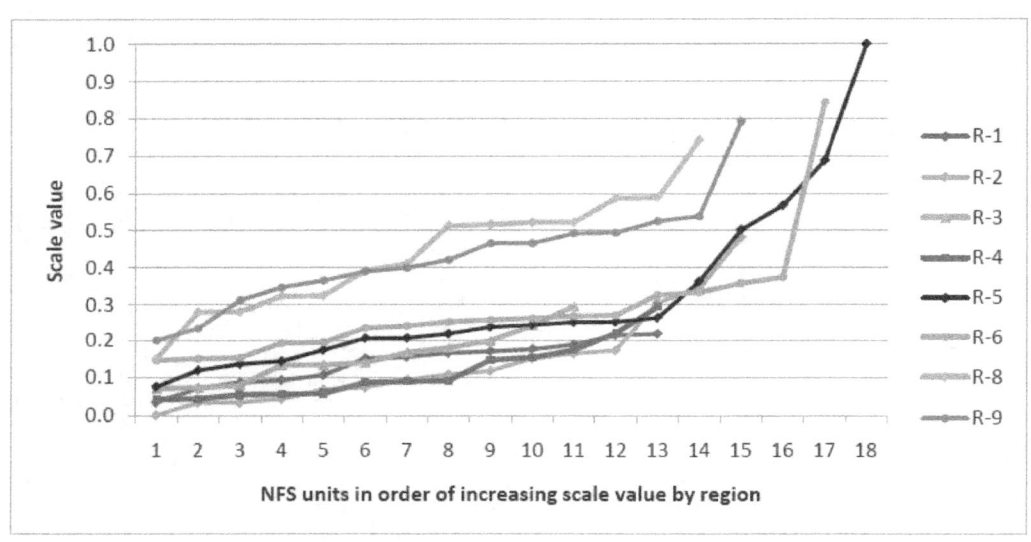

Figure 12a. Whole watersheds.

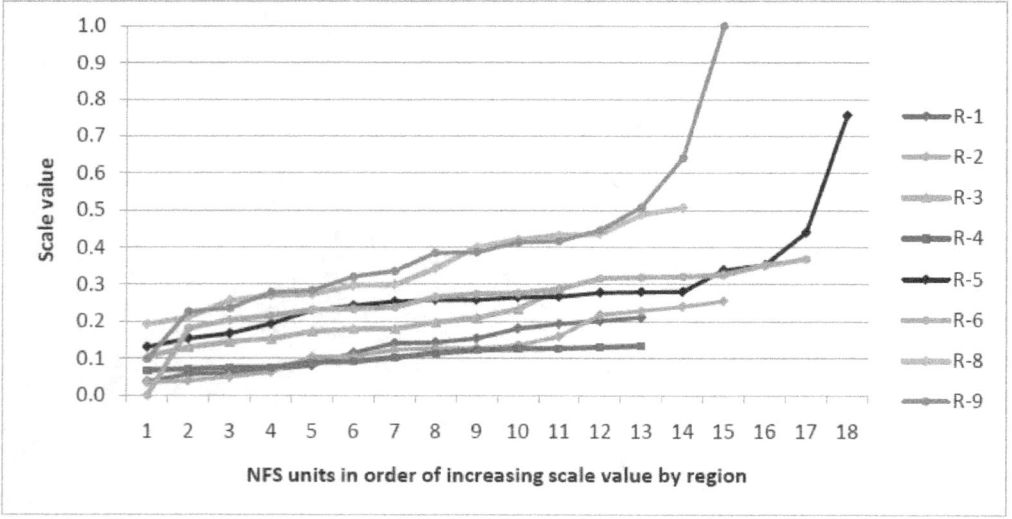

Figure 12b. Non-wilderness NFS parts of watersheds.

Regions 5 through 9 show a large range in scale value across their respective units, demonstrating a great variety in average risk across the units of those regions.

Restricting our purview now to the non-wilderness NFS parts of watersheds (figure 12b), we see that Regions 5 and 9 exhibit a much larger range in scale value among their respective units than do the other regions, but we also see that the unusually large ranges for these two regions are due to only a few units at the high-risk end of the scale. Figure 12b shows that all but nine of the 65 units with an average scale value above 0.2 are found in Regions 5 through 9; these 56 units are quite evenly spread among the four regions.

The reasons that Regions 5 through 9 contain a disproportionate share of the units at highest risk of watershed impairment on their non-wilderness NFS lands are seen in their relative levels of stressors and at-risk resources. As reported above, the following regions have on average the highest levels of the following stressors: population and livestock grazing (Region 8); road density and road-stream crossings (Region 6), roads in riparian areas and on steep slopes (Regions 5 and 6), cultivation (regions 8 and 9), and atmospheric deposition (Regions 8 and 9). And for resources at risk, the following regions have on average the highest levels: drinking water intakes (Region 5), water bodies (Regions 8 and 9); and density of wild and scenic river stretches (Regions 5, 6, and 9). For the other stressors and resources at risk, specific regions do not stand out when looking at regional averages.

Scale values for the individual NFS units, both for whole watersheds and non-wilderness NFS parts of watersheds, are listed in the accompanying online material (see footnote 20 for the website address). Similar results for non-NSF parts of watersheds are available in RWI.xls, which is also available online.

Changing the weights

The RWI.xls workbook was designed to easily produce results for different characterizations of risk to watershed condition than that summarized in figure 12. Alternative characterizations could involve a different environmental problem, a different balance between the stressor and at-risk resource components of the model, or a more limited set of stressors or at-risk resources. To see the effect of a new character-

ization of risk of impaired watershed condition, one merely needs to change the weights entered in the "Weights" worksheet of RWI.xls and then recompute the workbook. The only constraint on this process is that, at this point, it is limited to the set of indicators described in table 3.

As an example, we computed a new set of NFS unit scale values based on a more limited set of indicators, one that ignores the development and cultivation stressors (see table 3). Assigning zero weight to the development and cultivation stressors will affect some watersheds—those with high levels of development and cultivation—more than others. This characterization of risk of impaired watershed condition is of interest because it avoids any problems introduced by inaccuracies in the spatial data for the development and cultivation stressors, which in any case are stressors over which NFS managers are likely to have limited control. For this characterization the relative weights of the remaining stressors are maintained as they were in the original characterization (table 7) and all other features of the original characterization remain as described earlier, including the inclusion of the three environmental problems with weights of 0.6, 0.3, and 0.1, respectively, and the inclusion of both the stressor and at-risk-resource components of the model with weights of 0.7 and 0.3, respectively (table 7). We call this the "NFS-focused" characterization of risk of impaired watershed condition.

Figure 13 displays the results of this new characterization of risk of impaired watershed condition.[33] As with figure 12, the scale values depicted in figure 13 are computed with the NFS units scaled relative to the range in y_n across the full set of 116 NFS units. As in figure 12, the units are shown one per dot, arranged by region in order of increasing scale value from left to right. As seen in the figure, removing the development and cultivation stressors, which are some of the dominate causes or risk (found especially in Regions 5, 8 and 9), reduces the risk levels of the highest-risk watersheds, bringing them closer to some other watersheds and allowing the units to be more spread out across the range in scale value. Whereas before (with the full set of stressors) only 15 NFS units had a whole watershed scale value above 0.5, now 26 units have a scale value above 0.5. Or, restricting our

---

[33] A table in the accompanying online material contains the scale values for the individual NFS units based on the NFS-focused characterization of risk of impaired watershed condition (that are depicted in figure 13). This is done for summary scale values and for the individual problems, for NFS parts of watersheds. See footnote 20 for the website address.

Figure 13. Summary scale values of NFS units by region, using a NFS-focused set of indicators.

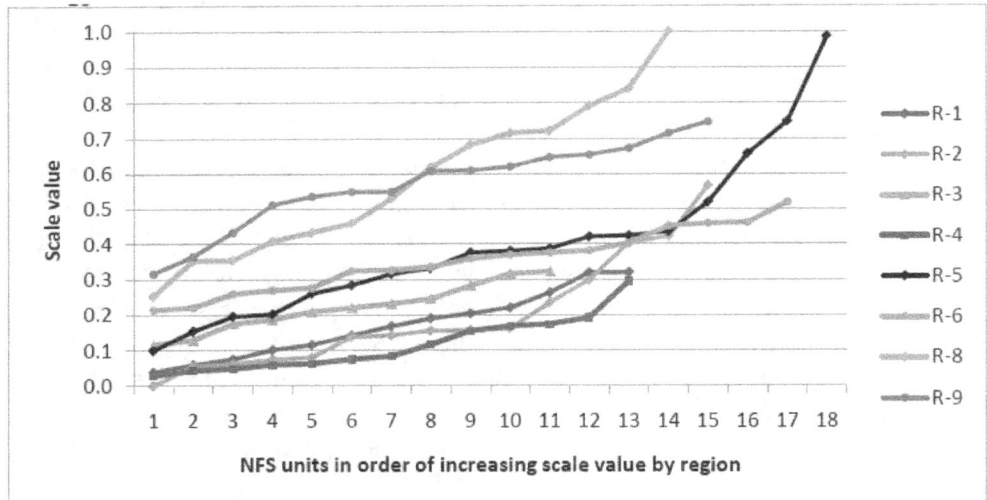

Figure 13a. Whole watersheds.

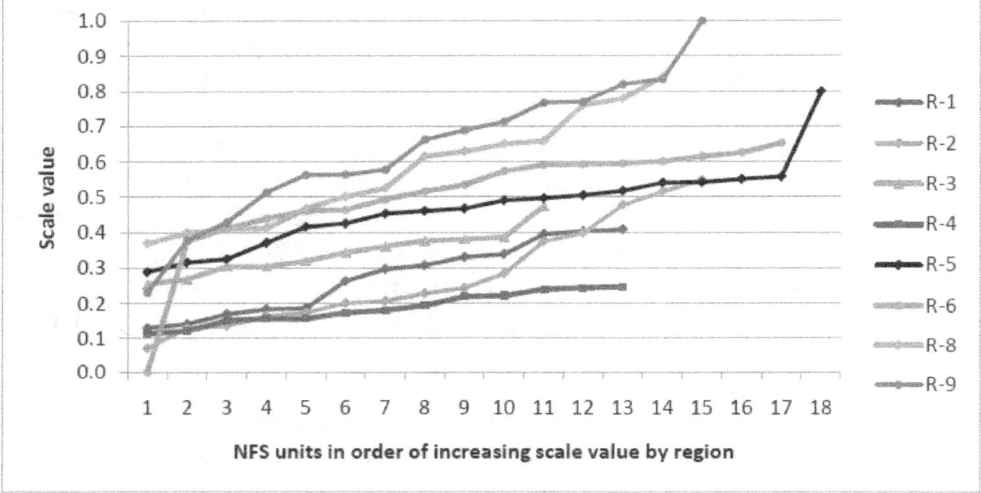

Figure 13b. Non-wilderness NFS parts of watersheds.

purview to non-wilderness NFS parts of watersheds, whereas only five NFS units in two regions had a scale value above 0.5 based on the full set of indicators, now 40 units spread across five regions have a scale value above 0.5. Interestingly, 21 of the 40 units are in the eastern regions and another 17 are in the West Coast regions. Thus, this look at the non-wilderness NFS parts of watersheds still shows a very unequal distribution among the regions of risk of impaired watershed condition, despite the fact that the effect of removing the development and cultivation stressors was felt largely in selected units of Regions 5, 8, and 9.

Comparison of figures 12 and 13 reveals that the two characterizations produce similar pictures of relative risk among the NFS units. For whole watersheds,

the Spearman rank order correlation between the two orderings is 0.96, and for non-wilderness NFS parts of watersheds the correlation is 0.95. This similarity in ranking generally holds for individual regions. However, the relative scale values may shift considerably when the development and cultivation stressors are removed from the set. For example, consider Region 6 for non-wilderness NFS parts of watersheds, shown in figure 14. The units of Region 6 are arranged from left to right in order of increasing scale value using the full set of indicators. As seen, using the NFS-focused set of indicators shifts the scale values upward; the scale values range from 0 to 0.37 using the full set and from 0 to 0.65 using the limited set. The general increase in scale value reflects the shifting of the scale following

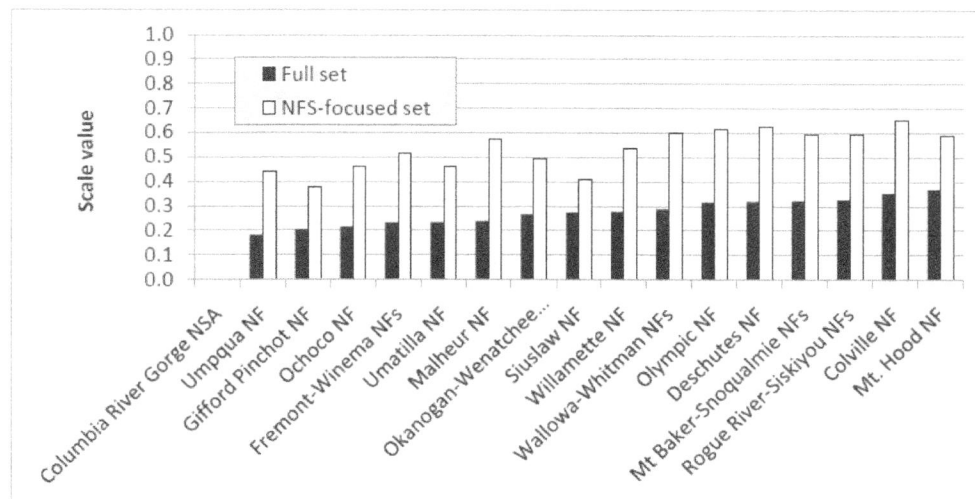

Figure 14. Comparison of summary scale values for NFS units in Region 6 using the full set and a NFS-management-focused set of indicators, non-wilderness NFS parts of watersheds.

removal of the effects of development and cultivation (these effects having caused units of other regions to capture the high end of the scale). However, as seen in figure 14, levels of development and cultivation, as we were able to measure those levels, are sufficiently prevalent and unequally distributed on NFS land in Region 6 to lead to some re-ordering of the units when stressors reflecting those impacts are removed from consideration.

Although the scale values of figures 12 and 13 were carefully derived and potentially are useful for decision making, we wish to emphasize that the full set of indicators of table 3 is limited by the availability of credible nationwide data, and that the weights of table 7 are based on our own judgment. If a process such as outlined herein were used to compare NFS units within regions, or watersheds within units, for the purpose of allocating budget or workloads, it should use indicators and weights chosen as a result of careful deliberation by the managers supervising the process.

Effect of erosivity

The use of erosivity to weight stressors affecting sediment is an option in RWI.xls. The erosivity value may be multiplied by the stressor value (v_i) before the scale value of the stressor is computed. In a separate analysis we used erosivity to weight the road, cultivation, grazing, mining, and fire hazard stressors, using the full set of indicators. The results for NFS unit scale values are presented in figure 15, which is comparable to figure 12 in all respects except for the erosivity weighting.

As expected given how erosivity varies across the regions—with Regions 8 and 9 having much higher erosivity values than the other regions (table 14)—the primary effect of weighting by erosivity is to increase the scale values of units in the eastern regions relative to the other regions. For example, considering only non-wilderness NFS parts of the watersheds, when not using erosivity 42 percent of the units with a scale value above 0.2 are in Regions 8 and 9 (figure 12), but when weighting by erosivity 70 percent of the units with a scale value above 0.2 are in those two regions (figure 15). We leave it to others to decide whether weighting by erosivity is an important addition to the assessment of risk of watershed impairment.

Summary of Major Findings__

We have summarized and analyzed a great deal of spatially explicit data, which reveals much about how watershed conditions vary across the country. These findings include the following:

- The NFS regions differ considerably in the degree of control that the agency has over the condition of the watersheds where the NFS units are found. In Regions 1, 4, 5, and 6 the NFS units tend to occupy about 44 percent of the watershed area; in Regions 2, 3, and 4 the NFS units tend to occupy about 34 percent of the watershed area; and in Regions 8 and 9 the NFS units tend to occupy only about 24 percent of the watershed area. Of course, within each region there is considerable variability, with some

Figure 15. Summary scale values of NFS units by region, with erosivity used to weight selected stressors.

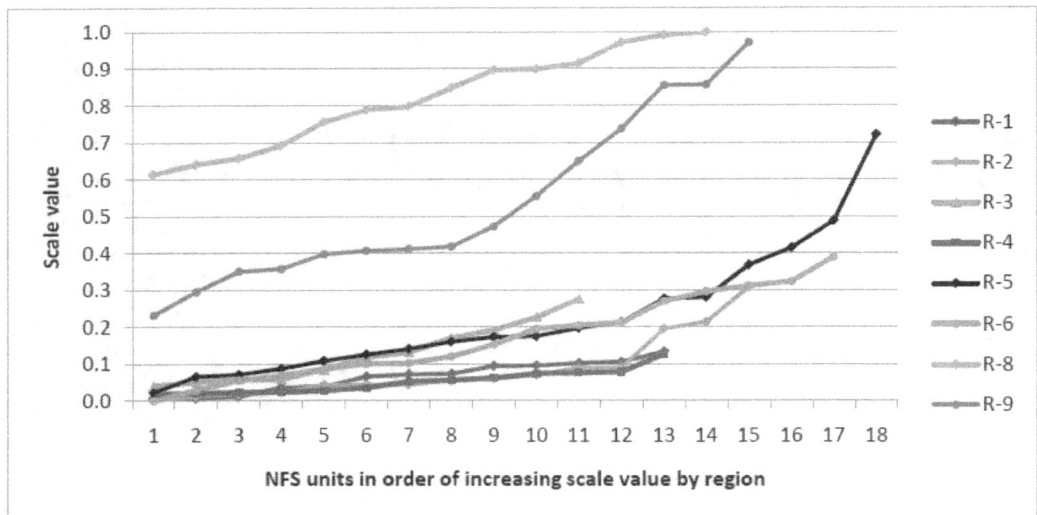

Figure 15a. Whole watersheds.

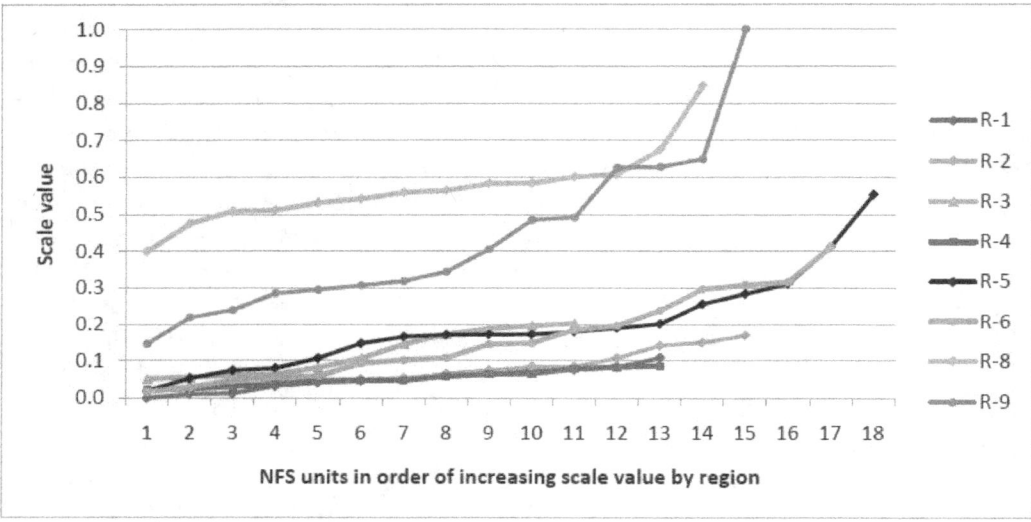

Figure 15b. Non-wilderness NFS parts of watersheds.

watersheds falling completely within a NFS unit and others containing very little NFS land.

- The regions differ greatly in the population density of their watersheds, ranging from 66 people per km² on average in Region 5 to less than 8 people per km² on average in Regions 1, 2, and 6. As with land ownership, there is great variation in population density among NFS units within a given region.

- Topography also varies greatly across the regions. The watersheds of the eastern regions tend to have the gentlest slopes, with roughly 60 percent of the watershed area having a slope less than 3 percent. The watersheds of Regions 5 and 6 tend to have

the steepest slopes; in these regions only about 15 percent of the slopes are less than 3 percent and 21 percent of the slopes exceed 45 percent.

- The regions differ considerably in vegetative cover. Extent of forest cover ranges from about 60 percent or more of the watershed area in Regions 6, 8, and 9 to about one-third of watershed area in Regions 2, 3 and 4. Extent of rangeland cover varies from two-thirds of watershed area in Region 3 and about 56 percent in Regions 2 and 4 to less than 8 percent in the eastern regions.

- Non-NFS parts of watersheds generally have greater road density, greater density of roads in riparian areas, and more road-stream crossings than do NFS parts of the watersheds, but NFS parts tend to have steeper slopes and a higher density of roads on very steep slopes. Based on regional averages for the four road stressors, and looking only at non-wilderness NFS parts of the watersheds (table 17), Regions 2 and 4 face relatively low road-related risk, followed by Region 1, whereas Region 6 faces high road-related risk. Of course, regional averages mask great diversity within regions.

- The densities of both grazing and confined animal feeding vary considerably across the regions. Watersheds of Region 8 tend to have the highest densities of both grazing and confined feeding, whereas watersheds in Regions 3, 4, and 6 typically have the lowest grazing densities and Regions 1, 4, 5, and 6 tend to have the lowest confined feeding densities (table 15).

- Sixty-one percent the watersheds have no listed aquatic T&E species, and 56 percent of the watersheds have no listed terrestrial species. Among the watersheds with listed species, the average number of listed T&E species per watershed is 1.8 for aquatic species and 1.9 for terrestrial species. Regions 6 and 8 tend to have the highest densities of listed species.

- At the watershed scale, stressors do not tend to be located in concert with at-risk resources. Across the watersheds of the West, the correlations of stressors to at-risk resources are positive but generally weak (Region 5 is an exception).

- The risk level distributions of the three problems are unimodal and skewed. For nutrients and toxics, most watersheds received a risk level of 1 (on a 6-point scale), whereas for sediment the mode is a risk level of 2. For all three problems, fewer than 17 percent of the watersheds fall at a risk level of 4 or higher (representing a scale value above 0.30). Thus, for all three problems, the upper two-thirds of the scale value range is occupied by only a few watersheds of highest risk. These findings apply to whole watersheds and also to non-wilderness NFS parts of watersheds.

- In terms of regional averages, Regions 5 through 9 have higher levels of risk than do Regions 1 to 4, whether we focus on whole watersheds or non-wilderness NFS parts of watersheds (see figures 10 and 12). Regions 5 through 9 tend to have both higher levels of stress and higher levels of at-risk resources than do Regions 1 through 4.

- Regional averages mask considerable variation within regions. At the NFS unit level, and focusing on non-wilderness NFS parts of watersheds and on the stressors most important on NFS land, this variation is smallest in Regions 1, 3, and 4 and greatest in Regions 6 and 9 (figure 13b).

- Although NFS parts of watersheds generally are at lower risk than non-NFS parts, this is not always the case. When non-wilderness NFS and non-NFS parts of watersheds across all regions are scaled together, making their scale values directly comparable, we find, for example, that while 36 percent of the non-wilderness NFS parts of watersheds are assigned to the lowest risk category, so also are 16 percent of the non-NFS parts. Thus, this 16 percent of the non-NFS parts of watersheds is at lower risk than 64 percent of the non-wilderness NFS parts (table 20). The 64 percent of the NFS parts at a risk level of 2 or higher are found in all regions, with 30 percent in Regions 5 and 6 and 35 percent in Regions 8 and 9.

Future Possibilities_____

Several improvements to this assessment are possible. The improvements fall into two groups: those possible without new data or models, and those that would require new data or models. Possible improvements that fall in the first group include the following: expanding the assessment to all watersheds in the coterminous United States; convening groups of watershed experts and managers to determine weights to be used in the assessment; separating private from other non-NFS land; accounting for the importance of location of water bodies within a watershed; accounting for resources at risk that are located downstream from the watershed at issue; and analyzing the relation of stressors to the EPA's list of impaired waters. Improvements that await new data or models include the following: adding stressors such as industrial sites and feedlots to improve the treatment of the three problems addressed herein; adding stressors such as water diversions or soil compaction to allow the assessment to address additional problems; adding additional resources at risk such as pristine stream stretches and highly valued recreational stream stretches; adapting data sources that rely on recent remote sensing efforts; and using models to improve the utility of stressors (for example, using a distributed erosion prediction model with our topography, soils, precipitation, and other data to improve the estimate of erosion potential).

Final Comments_____

The analysis confirmed what one would expect—that threats to watershed condition are generally much lower on NFS land than on the composite of other lands. The differences between NFS land and non-NFS lands that we measured would undoubtedly be greater if non-NFS lands had not included other protected lands. The substantial difference in risk of impaired watershed condition on NFS as opposed to non-NFS lands (figure 11) offers strong evidence that ecosystem processes and the goods and services that flow from those processes are under reduced risk on public lands, even if those lands are managed for multiple uses. Given the increase in development of private lands that is expected as the U.S. population continues to grow, the difference in risk of impaired watershed condition between public and private lands is likely to grow, thus increasing the value of the protected lands (Nie and Miller 2010).

Some of the differences between NFS and non-NFS lands were obvious from the start, such as the differences in cultivated area, population density, and housing density. Other differences were not so obvious, such as the much lower number of road-stream crossings or density of roads in riparian areas on NFS lands. However, some of the differences do not favor the NFS lands, such as the greater density of roads on steep slopes or of lands in fire condition class 3 on NFS lands (table 16).

The NFS units are not evenly spread across the range in scale value. For whole watersheds we find that only a small minority of the NFS units (15 out of 116) have a summary scale value in the top half of the scale value range (figure 12a). Ten of these 15 units are found in Regions 8 and 9 and four of the remaining five are in Region 5. Many factors contribute to this finding, but clearly among the most important of those

factors are population and related road and housing pressures, plus cultivation.

Knowing about the risk of impaired watershed condition for whole watersheds, when only portions the watersheds are in the NFS, is useful background knowledge that may influence what actions are taken on the NFS lands, but most pertinent for NFS managers is the information about non-wilderness NFS lands. Further, because development and cultivation stressors tend to pose the greatest risk of impairment but are the least amenable to change by public land management, perhaps the cleanest approach to comparing the NFS lands is to ignore the development and cultivation sets of stressors. When the weights placed on the stressors reflect this reasoning, many of the most worrisome watersheds (those with unusually dense human populations or cultivation) are no longer so worrisome, reducing the range in scale value and allowing more watersheds to move up in scale value (and thus in risk of impaired watershed condition). Considering only non-wilderness NFS parts of watersheds and using this restricted set of stressors, 40 NFS units have a summary scale value above 0.5, the midpoint of the scale (figure 13b). These 40 units include 21 of the 29 units in Regions 8 and 9, 17 of the 35 units in Regions 5 and 6, and only two of the 52 units in Regions 1 through 4. Clearly, risk of impaired watershed condition is not evenly spread across the regions. Of course, we must remember that the watersheds within an individual NFS unit may vary considerably in risk level; for example, it is not uncommon in units containing a watershed with a risk level of 5 or 6 to also contain watersheds with risk levels of 1 or 2.

We do not wish, however, to overstate the utility of the information we present. This assessment was intended primarily to provide an understanding of how watershed condition varies across large sections of the United States. The scale of the analysis restricted us to using only existing nationwide data sets, such that we were unable to include some variables that are undoubtedly important in assessing risk of watershed impairment (for example, feedlots, OHV use). Thus, the information included in this nationwide assessment may be too coarse or limited for local planning needs (although the data amassed here may serve as a starting point for others who wish to add more locally available data). For example, it is certainly possible that an assessment of risk of impaired watershed condition performed by a NFS unit would place heavy emphasis on a stressor not included here, such as OHV use. OHV use is unlikely to be strongly related to any of the stressors we used, causing the watershed ranking based on that local assessment to differ markedly from the ranking reported here. Finally, it is probably worth repeating the point that because of a lack of consistent, broad-scale data on soil quality, water quality, and aquatic species populations, this assessment produces a measure of the risk of watershed impairment, not a measure of actual watershed impairment.

Given that this analysis focuses on risk, rather than on objective measures of watershed condition or the degree to which ecosystem processes are compromised, one may ask: Is risk of a problem a sufficient basis for mitigation? The answer to this question is of course "no." Assessing risk is only the first step towards achieving a basis for mitigation. In addition, we must be sufficiently certain that the risk indeed has the potential to result in real harm, and we must be sufficiently convinced that the benefits of avoiding the harm outweigh the costs. Many studies, such as those cited in the Stressors subsection, have examined the relation between stressors and downstream, downslope, or down-wind environmental quality, and a good portion of them have found significant relations, although the strength of the relations undoubtedly varies by location. And still other studies have attempted to estimate the benefits and costs of mitigation efforts. Such studies should be consulted, and additional analyses would undoubtedly be helpful.

In addition to these additional steps, we must consider the scale at which mitigation decisions are best made. The appropriate scale for making decisions about on-the-ground mitigation actions is a much more regional or local scale than that represented by the huge land base assessed herein. National-level analyses provide a broad picture of the extent of a problem and some indication of how different areas of the country compare, and also provide a context and starting point for making local decisions, but they lack sufficient data and knowledge about local conditions to be a sufficient basis for on-the-ground management decisions. These more local analyses may take advantage of modeling efforts that are possible with more site-specific data (for an example, see Arabi and others 2006) and may involve local efforts to assign weights (for an example, see Shriver and Randhir 2006).

Literature Cited

Albasel, N.; Cottenie, A. 1985. Heavy metal contamination near major highways, industrial and urban areas in Belgian grassland. Water, Air, and Soil Pollution 24(1): 103-109.

Arabi, Mazdak; Govindaraju, Rao S.; Hantush, Mohamed M. 2006. Cost-effective allocation of watershed management practices using a genetic algorithm. Water Resources Research 42: W10429 (10421-10414).

Bartley, Rebecca; Corfield, Jeff P.; Abbott, Brett N.; Hawdon, Aaron A.; Wilkinson, Scott N. 2010. Impacts of improved grazing land management on sediment yields, part 1: hillslope processes. Journal of Hydrology 389(3-4): 237-248.

Belsky, A. J.; Matzke, A; Uselman, S. 1999. Survey of livestock influences on stream and riparian ecosystems in the western United States. Journal of Soil and Water Conservation 54(1): 419-431.

Benavides-Solorio, J. D.; MacDonald, L. H. 2001. Postfire runoff and erosion from simulated rainfall on small plots, Colorado Front Range. Hydrological Processes 15: 2391-2412.

Binkley, Dan; Brown, Thomas C. 1993. Forest practices as nonpoint sources of pollution in North America. Water Resources Bulletin 29(5): 729-740.

Brown, Thomas C.; Bergstrom, John C.; Loomis, John B. 2007. Defining, valuing, and providing ecosystem services. Natural Resources Journal 47(2): 331-376.

Brown, Thomas C.; Binkley, Dan. 1994. Effect of management on water quality in North American forests. Gen. Tech. Rep. RM-248. Fort Collins, CO: U.S. Department of Agriculture, Forest Service, Rocky Mountain Forest and Range Experiment Station. 27 p.

Cannon, S. H. ; Bigio, E. R. ; Mine, E. 2001. A process for fire-related debris flow initiation, Cerro Grande Fire, New Mexico. Hydrological Processes 15: 3011-3024.

Carpenter, S. R.; Caraco, N. F.; Correll, D. L.; Howarth, R. W.; Sharpley, A. N.; Smith, V. H. 1998. Nonpoint pollution of surface waters with phosphorus and nitrogen. Ecological Applications 8(3): 559-568.

Clingenpeel, Alan. 2003. A watershed analysis for the Ouachita National Forest (draft working copy). Hot Springs, AR: USDA Forest Service.

Courtney, Lisa A.; Clements, William H. 2002. Assessing the influence of water and substratum quality on benthic macroinvertebrate communities in a metal-polluted stream: an experimental approach. Freshwater Biology 47: 1766-1778.

Daly, C.; Neilson, R. P.; Phillips, D. L. 1994. A statistical-topographic model for mapping climatological precipitation over mountainous terrain. Journal of Applied Meteorology 33(2): 140-158.

Driscoll, Charles T.; Whitall, David; Aber, John; Boyer, Elizabeth; Castro, Mark; Cronan, Christopher; [and others]. 2003. Nitrogen pollution in the northeastern United States: sources, effects, and management options. Bioscience 53(4): 357-374.

Ebert, Udo; Welsch, Heinz. 2004. Meaningful environmental indices: a social choice approach. Journal of Environmental Economics and Management 47(2): 270-283.

Forman, Richard T. T.; Alexander, Lauren E. 1998. Roads and their major ecological effects. Annual Review of Ecology and Systematics 29: 207-231.

Gianessi, Leonard P.; Peskin, Henry M.; Puffer, C. A. 1986. National data base of nonurban-nonpoint-source discharges and their effect on the nation's water quality. Washington, DC: Resources for the Future.

Godt, Jonathan W. 2001. Landslide incidence and susceptibility in the conterminous United States. Open-File Report 97-289. Reston, VA: U.S. Geological Survey.

Graham, Russell T., editor. 2003. Hayman Fire case study. Gen. Tech. Rep. RMRS-GTR-114. Ogden, UT: U.S. Department of Agriculture, Forest Service, Rocky Mountain Research Station. 396 p.

Hansen, William F. 2001. Identifying stream types and management implications. Forest Hydrology and Management 143(1): 39-46.

Hoffman, Ryan S.; Capel, Paul D.; Larson, Steven J. 2000. Comparison of pesticides in eight U.S. urban streams. Environmental Toxicology and Chemistry 19(9): 2249–2258.

Hudy, Mark; Thieling, Teresa M.; Gillespie, Nathaniel; Smith, Eric P. 2008. Distribution, status, and land use characteristics of subwatersheds within the native range of brook trout in the eastern United States. North American Journal of Fish Management 28(4): 1069-1085.

Johnson, S. R.; Gary, H. L.; Ponce, S. L. 1978. Range cattle impacts on stream water quality in the Colorado Front Range. Research Note RM-359. Fort Collins, CO: U.S. Department of Agriculture, Forest Service, Rocky Mountain Forest and Range Experiment Station.

Jones, K. B.; Heggem, Daniel T.; Wade, Timothy G.; Neale, Anne C.; Ebert, Donald; Nash, Maliha; [and others]. 2000. Assessing landscape condition relative to water resources in the western United States: A strategic approach. Environmental Monitoring and Assessment 64: 227-245.

Jones, K. Bruce; Neale, Anne C.; Nash, Maliha S.; Remortel, Rick D. Van; Wickham, James D.; Riitters, Kurt H.; [and others]. 2001. Predicting nutrient and sediment loadings to streams from landscape metrics: a multiple watershed study from the United States Mid-Atlantic region. Landscape Ecology 16: 301-312.

Jones, K. Bruce; Ritters, Kurt H.; Wichham, James D.; Tankersley, Roger D., Jr.; O'Neill, Robert B.; Chaloud, Deborah J.; [and others]. 1997. An ecological assessment of the United States Mid-Atlantic region: A landscape atlas. EPA/600/R-97/130. Washington, DC: U.S. Environmental Protection Agency.

Kauffman, J. Boone; Krueger, W. C. 1984. Livestock impacts on riparian ecosystems and streamside management implications ... a review. Journal of Range Management 37(5): 430-438.

Kelly, J.; Thornton, I.; Simpson, P. R. 1996. Urban geochemistry: a study of the influence of anthropogenic activity on the heavy metal content of soils in traditionally industrial and non-industrial areas of Britain. Environmental Geochemistry 11(1-2): 363-370.

Luce, Charles H.; Black, Thomas A. 1999. Sediment production from forest roads in western Oregon. Water Resources Research 35(8): 2561-2570.

Mallin, Michael A. 2000. Impacts of industrial animal production on rivers and estuaries. American Scientist 88(1): 26-37.

Moody, J. A.; Martin, D. A. 2001. Initial hydrologic and geomorphic response following a wildfire in the Colorado Front Range. Earth Surface Processes and Landforms 26: 1049-1070.

Mueller, David K.; Helsel, Dennis R. 1996. Nutrients in the nation's waters: too much of a good thing? Circular 1136. Denver, CO: U.S. Geological Survey.

Neary, Daniel G.; Ryan, Kevin C.; DeBano, Leonard F. 2005. Wildland fire in ecosystems: effects of fire on soil and water. Gen. Tech. Rep. RMRS-GTR-42-vol. 4. Ogden, UT: U.S. Department of Agriculture, Forest Service, Rocky Mountain Research Station. 250 p.

Nie, Martin; Miller, Char. 2010. National forest management and private land development: historical, political, and planning considerations. Society and Natural Resources 23(7): 669-678.

Omernik, J. M. 1977. Nonpoint source-stream nutrient level relationships: a nationwide study. 600/3-77-105. Corvalis, OR: Environmental Research Laboratory, Office of Research and Development, U. S. Environmental Protection Agency.

Paul, Michael J.; Meyer, Judy L. 2001. Streams in the urban landscape. Annual Review of Ecology and Systematics 32: 333-365.

Pouyat, Richard V.; McDonnell, Mark J.; Pickett, S. T. A. 1995. Soil characteristics of oak stands along an urban-rural land-use gradient. Journal of Environmental Quality 24(3): 516-526.

Radbruch-Hall, Dorothy H.; Colton, Roger B.; Davies, William E.; Lucchitta, Ivo; Skipp, Betty A.; Varnes, David J. 1982. Landslide overview map of the conterminous United States. U.S. Geological Survey Professional Paper 1183. Washington, DC: US Government Printing Office.

Reeves, Gordon H.; Hohler, David B.; Larsen, David P.; Busch, David E.; Kratz, Kim; Reynolds, Keith; [and others]. Undated. Aquatic and riparian effectiveness monitoring plan for the Northwest Forest Plan. Portland, OR: Regional Ecosystem Office, Northwest Forest Plan. Available: http://www.reo.gov/monitoring/reports/watershed/aremp/aremp.htm.

Renard, K. G.; Foster, G. R.; Weesies, G. A.; McCool, D. K.; Yoder, D. C. 1997. Predicting soil erosion by water: a guide to conservation planning with the Revised Universal Soil Loss Equation (RUSLE). Ag. Handb. 703. Washington, DC: U. S. Department of Agriculture, Agricultural Research Service.

Roline, Richard A. 1988. The effects of heavy metals pollution on the upper Arkansas River on the distribution of aquatic macroinvertebrates. Hydrobiology 160: 3-8.

Rosner, Ulrike. 1998. Effects of historical mining activities on surface water and groundwater—an example from northwest Arizona. Environmental Geology 33(4): 224-230.

Schmidt, Kirsten M.; Menakis, James P.; Hardy, Colin C.; Hann, Wendel J.; Bunnell, David L. 2000. Development of coarse-scale spatial data for wildland fire and fuel management. Gen. Tech. Rep. RMRS-GTR-87. Fort Collins, CO: U.S. Department of Agriculture, Forest Service, Rocky Mountain Research Station. 41 p. + CD.

Shields, Deborah; Brown, Douglas D.; Brown, Thomas C. 1995. The distribution of abandoned and inactive mines on National Forest System lands. Gen. Tech. Rep. RM-260. Fort Collins, Colorado: U.S. Department of Agriculture, Forest Service, Rocky Mountain Forest and Range Experiment Station. 195 p.

Shriver, Deborah M.; Randhir, Timothy O. 2006. Integrating stakeholder values with multiple attributes to quantify watershed performance. Water Resources Research 42: W08435 (08431-08415).

Smith, Elizabeth R.; Tran, Liem T.; O'Neill, Robert V. 2003. Regional vulnerability assessment for the mid-Atlantic region: Evaluation of integration methods and assessment results. Research Triangle Park, NC: U.S. Environmental Protection Agency.

Smith, Richard A.; Alexander, Richard B.; Wolman, M. Gordon. 1987. Water-quality trends in the nation's rivers. Science 235: 1607-1615.

U.S. Environmental Protection Agency. 1990. National water quality inventory: 1988 report to Congress. EPA-841-R-97-008. Washington, DC: U.S. Environmental Protection Agency.

U.S. Forest Service. 2000a. East-wide watershed assessment protocol for forest plan amendment, revision, and implementation. Atlanta, GA: U.S. Department of Agriculture, Forest Service, Southern Region.

U.S. Forest Service. 2000b. Rating watershed condition: reconnaissance level assessment for the National Forests of the Pacific Southwest Region. On file with: U.S. Department of Agriculture, Forest Service, Pacific Southwest Region.

U.S. Water Resources Council. 1978. The nation's water resources 1975-2000. Washington, DC: U. S. Government Printing Office.

Wickham, James D.; Riitters, Kurt H.; Wade, Timothy G.; Jones, K. Bruce. 2005. Evaluating the relative roles of ecological regions and land-cover composition for guiding establishment of nutrient criteria. Landscape Ecology 20: 791-798.

Wischmeier, W. H.; Smith, D. D. 1978. Predicting rainfall erosion loss: a guide to conservation planning. Ag. Handb. 537. Washington, DC: U. S. Department of Agriculture.

Wohl, Neil E.; Carline, Robert F. 1996. Relations among riparian grazing, sediment loads, macroinvertebrates, and fishes in three central Pennsylvania streams. Canadian Journal of Fisheries and Aquatic Sciences 53: 260-266.

Zhou, P.; Ang, B. W.; Poh, K. L. 2006. Comparing aggregating methods for constructing the composite environmental index: an objective measure. Ecological Economics 59(3): 305-311.

Appendix A: Watershed Area, Elevation, and Ownership

The watersheds range in size from 27 to 1652 km², with a mean of 511 km². Mean watershed surface area varies across the regions from 418 km² in Region 5 to 659 km² in Region 3 (table A1). The NFS portions of the watersheds range in size from about 1 to 1175 km², with a mean of 187 km². Mean surface area of the NFS portions of the watersheds varies across the regions from 110 km² in Region 8 to 231 km² in Region 3. The non-NFS portions of the watersheds, for the subset of watersheds with non-NFS land, range in size from below 1 to 1542 km², with a mean of 336 km². Mean non-NFS surface area varies across the regions from 234 km² in Region 5 to 433 km² in Region 3.

Across all 3672 watersheds, mean elevation ranges from -67 to 4410 m, with a mean of 1371 m (table A2). Mean elevation varies across the regions from 290 m in Region 8 to 2134 m in Region 2. Mean elevation of the NFS portions of the watersheds is greater than that of the non-NFS portions of the watersheds in all regions; mean NFS elevation exceeds mean non-NFS elevation by from 119 m in Region 9 to 805 m in Region 2; this difference averages 547 m across all watersheds. A cleaner comparison of NFS and non-NFS portions of the watersheds than that presented in table A2 is possible if we restrict the watershed set to the 3541 watersheds with both classes of land ownership. This comparison is shown in figure A1, where we see that the difference between the mean elevation of NFS portions of the watersheds and the mean elevation of non-NFS portions diminishes with overall elevation as we move away from the central Rocky Mountains, with the smallest differences found in the eastern regions. Also shown in figure A1 is the percent of the watersheds of each region where the elevation of the

NFS portion exceeds that of the non-NFS portion. For example, the elevation of the NFS portion exceeds that of the non-NFS portion in 89% of the watersheds of Region 1.

Within each NFS region, watersheds vary across the land ownership spectrum, from those with only 1% of their land in the NFS (our cutoff for inclusion) to watersheds that are completely NFS land. The NFS portion of the watersheds tends to be smaller than the non-NFS portion; across the full set of watersheds, the median NFS portion is only 32%. However, the regions differ markedly in how much of their watersheds are typically in the NFS and fall into three groups, as shown in figure A2, which presents the cumulative proportions of watersheds in each region with given levels of NFS land in the watersheds.[1] The figure shows, for each region, the proportion of the watersheds that contain less than any given percent NFS, or, in other words, the proportion of the watersheds that are at least a given percent NFS. For example, the dotted line in the figure, which is at the 50% point along the horizontal axis, intersects the lines for the two eastern regions at about 0.85, indicating that about 15% of the watersheds are greater than one-half NFS land. However, in Regions 2 and 3 about 30% of the watersheds are greater than one-half NFS land, and in Regions 1, 4, 5, and 6 about 55% of the watersheds are greater than one-half NFS land (with Region 4 slightly above the other three regions in the vicinity of the dotted 50% line). Thus, the regions differ considerably in how much control the agency tends to have over the condition of the watersheds, with the regions in the northern Rockies and along the West coast tending to have the greatest control.

---

[1] Figure A2 is produced by arranging the watersheds of each region in order of increasing percentage of the watershed in the NFS.

Table A1. Surface area of watersheds by NFS region (km²).

	NFS Region									All watersheds
	1	2	3	4	5	6	8	9		
Whole watersheds[a]										
Minimum	65	89	112	58	106	27	85	74		27
Maximum	1116	1478	1432	1652	1295	1435	1324	1347		1652
Mean	482	565	659	506	418	465	489	540		510
NFS parts of watersheds[a]										
Minimum	3	4	5	<1	1	2	2	2		<1
Maximum	943	1175	1113	1175	808	909	516	760		1175
Mean	209	190	231	205	189	214	110	139		187
Non-NFS parts of watersheds[b]										
Minimum	0	3	0	0	0	1	0	7		0
Maximum	1061	1365	1379	1542	973	1220	1255	1131		1542
Mean	308	382	433	319	234	259	381	402		336

[a] 3672 watersheds.
[b] 3541 watersheds.

Table A2. Elevation of watersheds by NFS region (m above sea level).

	NFS Region									All watersheds
	1	2	3	4	5	6	8	9		
Whole watersheds[a]										
Minimum	266	432	283	512	-67	-1	-14	0		-67
Maximum	3898	4397	4168	4210	4410	4394	2037	1915		4410
Mean[c]	1474	2134	1795	2018	1270	1088	290	376		1371
NFS parts of watersheds[a]										
Minimum	288	462	398	512	-1	0	-3	64		-3
Maximum	3898	4397	4014	4210	4410	3746	2012	1882		4410
Mean[c]	1728	2667	2011	2325	1583	1300	383	452		1718
Non-NFS parts of watersheds[b]										
Minimum	266	432	283	513	-67	-1	-14	0		-67
Maximum	3466	4370	4168	4192	4403	4394	2037	1915		4403
Mean[c]	1279	1863	1678	1808	1012	906	264	350		1171

[a] 3672 watersheds.
[b] 3541 watersheds.
[c] Area-weighted mean.

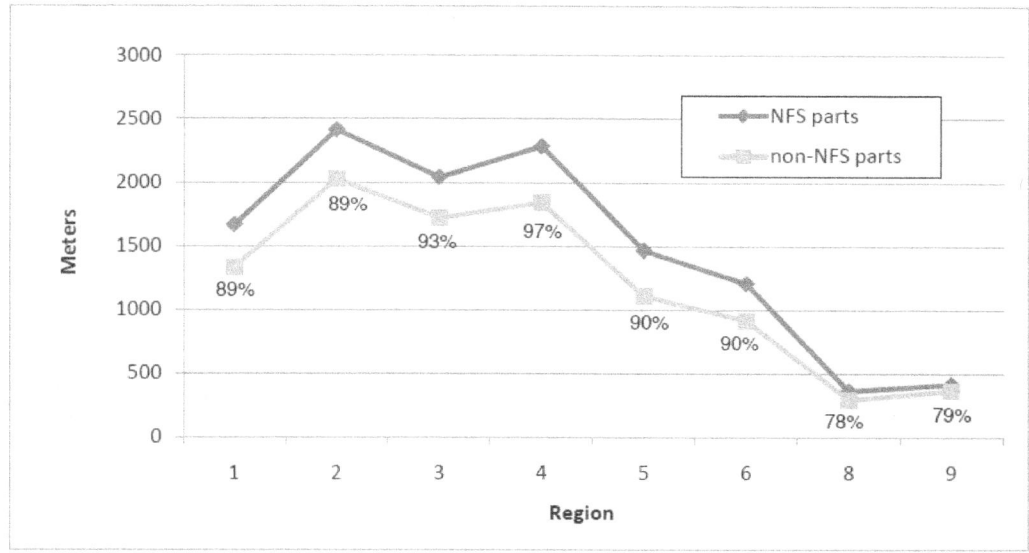

Figure A1. Mean elevation of portions of watersheds (percentages are of the number of watersheds within a region with average NFS elevation > average non-NFS elevation).

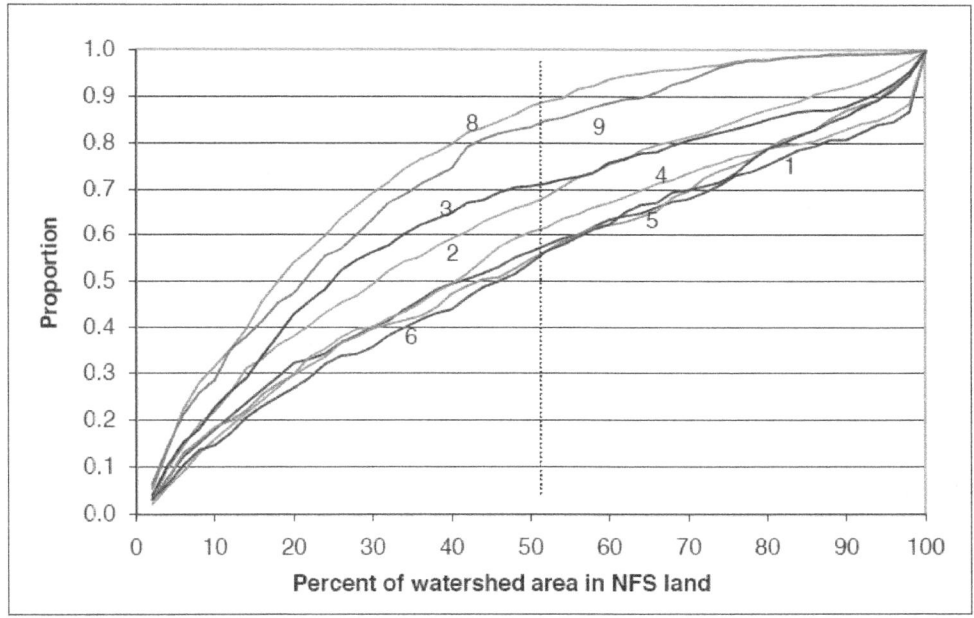

Figure A2. Cumulative proportion of watersheds with given levels of NFS land (numbers indicate NFS regions, using ALP boundaries for all regions).

Appendix B: Incidence of Threatened and Endangered Species

Listed threatened and endangered (T&E) species (aquatic and non-aquatic) are included as at-risk resources in the above analysis of risks of impaired watershed condition. The T&E species counts were provided by NatureServe in early 2010 for all 3672 whole watersheds. NatureServe also provided information about non-listed species. This section presents more detail about the NatureServe data, both listed and non-listed, for the watersheds.

Methods

Counts of the number of T&E species in each of the 3672 whole watersheds were computed by Nature-Serve using watershed boundaries that we provided to them for this project. NatureServe overlaid the watershed boundaries on its "Element Occurrence" (EO) species location data, which includes both global level (range-wide) tracking data developed centrally at NatureServe as well as state level tracking data provided by natural heritage programs across the United States.[2]

The T&E data include all federal status species. Federal status species are those that have been assigned the following status designations by the U.S. Fish and Wildlife Service under the Endangered Species Act: listed endangered, listed threatened, proposed endangered, proposed threatened, candidate, special concern, proposed for delisting, listed endangered or threatened because of similarity of appearance, proposed endangered or threatened because of similarity of appearance, essential experimental population, and nonessential experimental population. In our data, these different status designations are combined into two groups: listed (both endangered and threatened) and non-listed (all other categories).

It is important to notice that the species counts provided by NatureServe are counts per watershed. Thus, the data do not indicate which species are found in a watershed and may include the same species in different watersheds. We have summarized the data for larger areas, such as NFS regions, by simply summing across watersheds. We have no way to know how many different species are included in the total count for a multi-watershed area. Across all 3672 watersheds the total count is 5151, 85% of which (4399) is for listed species.

The EO is the mapping unit developed by Natural Heritage Programs for documenting the distribution of species populations. Formally defined as "an area of land and/or water in which a species or natural community is, or was, present," an element occurrence ideally reflects species population units, either a distinct population, part of a population (sub-population), or a group of populations (meta-population).

The completeness of the EO data varies among species. As NatureServe explains, the data are particularly strong and complete for terrestrial and freshwater vertebrate species and vascular plants, and for entities with T&E status. Many invertebrate groups are completely tracked, but the data on these elements continue to expand. The non-vascular plant data (lichens, mosses, liverworts and hornworts, and fungi) are being actively developed and EOs for these groups will expand over the next few years.[3,4]

EOs were filtered out of the analysis that are known to be extirpated or that have not been last observed since 1970. One exception is with the Washington animal data—the Washington DFW only tracks records observed no later than 1976.

The accuracy of the mapping of EO polygons varies and is categorized in the NatureServe database as high, medium, or low. Using this accuracy information, and in light of the fact that EOs are nearly always considerably smaller than 5th-level watersheds, the following overlap rules were applied for the spatial

---

[2] NatureServe does not have precise location data in-house for Arizona, Massachusetts, New Hampshire, and Pennsylvania. To fill those data gaps for this analysis, each of those state programs intersected their EOs of federal status species with the watershed layer we provided (and NatureServe then sent to the states). The results of these separate state-level analyses were then incorporated with the EO overlay results for the rest of the country.

[3] NatureServe performs a data exchange with each Heritage Program in the United States on an annual basis, but NatureServe does not guarantee the currentness or completeness of any data provided. Because data are constantly being revised and new data are constantly being developed, the data presented here may soon be out of date.

[4] NatureServe provided a detailed state-by-state list of the data limitations, which is available by contacting the authors.

overlay in order for a species to be counted for a watershed. For EO records that were assigned a high mapping accuracy value, a species was counted for a watershed if there was any intersection at all between the watershed and the EO polygon. For EO records that were assigned a medium to low mapping accuracy value, or for which a mapping accuracy value has not yet been assigned (the majority of the data fell into this category), a species was counted for a watershed if 25% or more of the area of its representative EO(s) overlapped with the watershed.[5]

NatureServe distinguishes between two habitat categories, aquatic associated and terrestrial associated, depending on whether a habitat is known to "contribute significantly to the survival or reproduction of the species at some point in its lifecycle," which does not necessarily mean that the habitat is critical to a species' survival. These two habitat categories are not mutually exclusive, and many species are listed as belonging to both categories. For example, birds that utilize aquatic habitats for hunting or nesting, such as the osprey, would be assigned to the "aquatic associated" category even though they do not actually live in the water and are also assigned to the terrestrial associated category. However, not all species have as yet been assigned to one of these two habitat categories. Unclassified species are listed below as "unassigned."

Because the collection of aquatic associated species includes many species not principally reliant on water flows, aquatic species were also categorized based on their taxonomic group in a category that NatureServe calls aquatic "obligate" species. Aquatic obligate species spend their lives in the water and do not include plants (which can be adaptable to different hydrologic regimes in different areas), amphibians, or reptiles such as turtles (some of which are more aquatic than others). Aquatic obligate species belong to the following taxonomic groups: crayfishes; fairy, clam, and tadpole shrimps; freshwater and anadromous fishes; freshwater mussels; and freshwater snails.[6]

Results

Table B1 lists the species counts by region for the different listing and habitat categories described above. Note that if the total number of species (those in the "All" rows of the table) is less than the sum of aquatic associated and terrestrial associated rows, it is because one or more species has been listed as both aquatic associated and terrestrial associated. This double counting occurs with listed species in 819 watersheds and with non-listed species in 89 watersheds.

As seen in table B1, most (85%) of the T&E species count data pertain to listed species. Across all watersheds the total species count for listed species is 4399, with 2357 for aquatic associated species, 2933 for terrestrial associated species, and 134 for unassigned species. Of the total count of 2357 for aquatic associated species, 45% (1049) is for aquatic obligate species.

Region 8 has the largest count of listed species, with 978, or 22% of the total, followed by Region 6 with 19% (table B1). These two regions have the largest counts of aquatic associated, aquatic obligate, and terrestrial associated species. At the other end of the spectrum, Region 2 has the smallest count of listed species, with 224, or 5% of the total, followed by Region 9 with 6%.

Only 2048 watersheds, 56% of the full set of watersheds, have a listed species. Further, the regions vary greatly in the likelihood that a watershed has a listed T&E species; across the regions, the percentage of watersheds with at least one listed species ranges from 36% for Region 2 to 77% for Region 6 (figure B1). For aquatic associated species, only 39% of the watersheds have a listed species, with regional percentages varying from 24% for Region 9 to 61% for Region 6 (figure B1). And for aquatic obligate species, only 19% of the watersheds have a listed species, with regional percentages varying from 6% for Regions 2 and 9 to 32% for Region 6. Finally, for terrestrial associated species, 46% of the watersheds have a listed species, with regional percentages varying from 27% for Region 1 to

---

[5] Because mapped territories are nearly always considerably smaller than 10-digit watersheds, it was not considered necessary to apply the converse of this rule, where a mapped territory would be reported if it covered at least 25% of the total area of the watershed.

[6] In the original NatureServe data, some species in the aquatic obligate taxonomic groups were not also listed as aquatic associated species, causing the number of aquatic obligate species to sometimes exceed the number of aquatic species. This was corrected by entering aquatic in the habitat field for all species included in the aquatic obligate taxonomic group.

Table B1. T&E species counts by region.

Variable	NFS Region 1	2	3	4	5	6	8	9	All watersheds
Number of watersheds									
All	494	460	356	624	433	466	489	350	3672
With ≥ one listed species	242	167	253	311	202	361	362	150	2048
With ≥ one species (listed or non-listed)	245	179	256	341	300	398	379	156	2254
Numbers of species (sum of counts across all watersheds in region)									
All categories (listed and non-listed)	325	241	761	532	850	1035	1089	318	5151
Listed									
All	316	224	648	466	663	832	978	272	4399
Aquatic associated	225	144	314	239	287	467	562	119	2357
Terrestrial associated	183	184	396	382	419	577	576	216	2933
Unassigned	9	9	7	7	52	17	28	5	134
Aquatic obligate	124	31	156	76	122	238	268	34	1049
Not assigned aquatic[a]	91	80	334	227	376	365	416	153	2042
Non-listed									
All	9	17	113	66	187	203	111	46	752
Aquatic associated	1	1	28	35	68	106	71	46	356
Terrestrial associated	3	13	85	42	142	105	43	19	452
Unassigned	5	3	0	20	2	1	2	0	33
Aquatic obligate	0	1	27	1	0	33	52	18	132

[a] Either unassigned (could be terrestrial or aquatic) or terrestrial but not also aquatic.

65% for Region 3 (with Regions 6 and 8 close by at 64% and 62%, respectively) (figure B1).

Figure B2 shows the species counts per watershed for watersheds with at least one listed T&E species for the respective species category. For example, in Region 3 there are 253 watersheds with at least one listed aquatic associated species (39% of the total of 648 watersheds). Across these 253 watersheds the average listed aquatic associated T&E species count is 2.56 per watershed. As seen in figure B2, Region 5 has the highest concentration of listed T&E species (3.28 per watershed among the 202 watersheds with at least one listed species) and listed terrestrial associated T&E species (2.89 per watershed among the 145 watersheds with at least one listed terrestrial species), whereas Region 8 has the highest concentration of listed aquatic associated T&E species (2.38 per watershed among the 236 watersheds with at least one listed aquatic species).[7] The lowest concentrations of listed T&E species occur in Regions 1, 2, and 4.

Of the 116 units, only four have no listed species in the watersheds containing NFS land, and only eight have no listed aquatic species. For example, 17 of the 18 watersheds where land of the Bitterroot National Forest is found have at least one listed T&E species. A table in Section C of the material posted on the website (see footnote 20) lists by NFS unit the number of watersheds that have listed T&E species.

Among the 116 NFS units, the median number of listed aquatic or terrestrial species is 4, and the median total number of listed species is 7. The George Washington-Jefferson National Forests have the greatest number of listed aquatic species (35), and the San Bernardino National Forest has the greatest number of listed terrestrial species (32). The George Washington-Jefferson National Forests also have the greatest total number of listed species (53). A table in the accompanying online material lists by NFS unit the number of separate T&E species found in the watersheds containing NFS land.

Maps in the accompanying online material show the number of listed T&E species for each of the 3672 watersheds, for aquatic and terrestrial species separately.

---

[7] Concentrations vary considerably across NFS units within a region. For example, the high concentrations in Region 5 are due largely to just a few of the 18 NFS units in the region. For total (aquatic plus terrestrial) counts of listed species, only three national forests (the Angeles, Cleveland, and San Bernardino National Forests, all in southern California) have concentrations above 3 species per watershed.

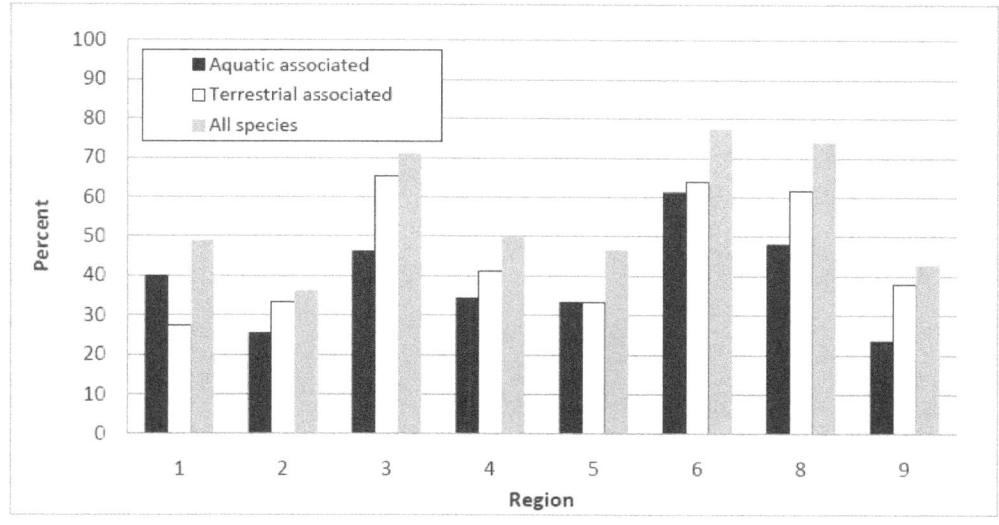

Figure B1. Percent of watersheds with at least one listed species.

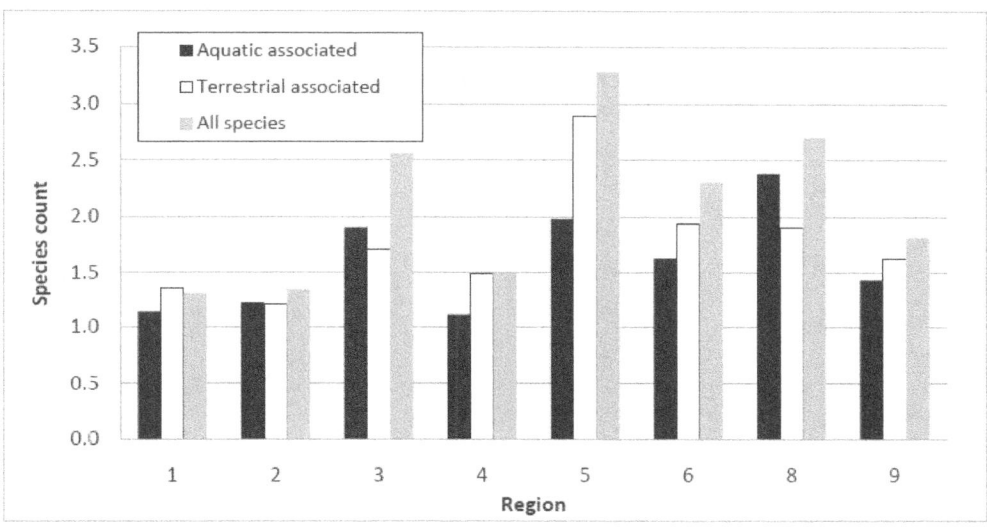

Figure B2. Average number of listed species per watershed among watersheds with at least one listed species.